Trello

for Beginners

Master Task Management with Ease

Kiet Huynh

Table of Contents

CHAPTER I
Getting Started with Trello

1.1 What is Trello?

About Trello
What's behind the boards.

The way your team works is unique – so is Trello.

Trello is the flexible work management tool where teams can ideate plans, collaborate on projects, organize workflows, and track progress in a visual, productive, and rewarding way. From brainstorm to planning to execution, Trello manages the big milestones and the day-to-day tasks of working together and getting things done.

In today's fast-paced world, managing tasks effectively is crucial for both individuals and teams. Whether you are working on a personal project, collaborating with a team, or organizing your daily activities, having a structured approach can significantly boost productivity. This is where Trello comes in—a simple yet powerful tool designed to help users visually manage their tasks and workflows.

The Basics of Trello

Trello is a web-based project management application that allows users to organize and track tasks using a system of boards, lists, and cards. Developed by Fog Creek Software in

2011 and later acquired by Atlassian in 2017, Trello has grown into one of the most popular task management tools, widely used by individuals, businesses, and teams worldwide.

Trello operates on the Kanban methodology, which provides a visual representation of work progress. The system is highly flexible and can be customized to fit different workflows, whether for project management, event planning, personal productivity, or even household organization.

Key Components of Trello

To understand Trello's functionality, it's essential to become familiar with its three core components:

- **Boards**: A board represents a project or workspace. It is the highest level of organization in Trello, where all tasks and activities related to a specific project are managed.

- **Lists**: Each board contains multiple lists that represent different stages of a workflow. These lists help structure tasks by categorizing them based on progress, such as "To-Do," "In Progress," and "Completed."

- **Cards**: Cards are the fundamental units of Trello, representing individual tasks. Users can move cards across lists as tasks progress, assign them to team members, add due dates, attach files, and more.

These three elements form the foundation of Trello's user-friendly yet powerful system, making it easy to organize work in a way that suits individual or team needs.

Why Use Trello?

Trello is widely recognized for its simplicity, flexibility, and collaboration features. Here are a few reasons why Trello stands out as a preferred task management tool:

1. User-Friendly Interface

Trello's drag-and-drop functionality, intuitive layout, and minimal learning curve make it accessible to users of all experience levels. Unlike traditional project management software that can feel overwhelming, Trello keeps things simple and visually appealing.

2. Highly Customizable

Users can customize Trello boards to match their workflow. Whether you need a personal task manager, a team collaboration tool, or an advanced project management system, Trello adapts to various use cases.

3. Real-Time Collaboration

Trello enables seamless collaboration by allowing multiple users to work on the same board simultaneously. Team members can comment on tasks, mention colleagues, and receive real-time updates, making remote work and project coordination effortless.

4. Integration with Other Tools

Trello integrates with a variety of productivity tools such as Google Drive, Slack, Microsoft Teams, and Jira, allowing users to streamline their workflows by connecting different applications within Trello.

5. Available on Multiple Platforms

Trello is accessible via web browsers, desktop applications (Windows and macOS), and mobile apps (iOS and Android), ensuring that users can manage their tasks anytime, anywhere.

How Trello is Used Across Different Fields

Trello's flexibility makes it suitable for a variety of use cases, including:

- **Project Management**: Teams use Trello to track project progress, assign tasks, and collaborate efficiently.

- **Content Planning**: Writers, marketers, and designers use Trello to plan blog posts, social media content, and design projects.

- **Software Development**: Agile teams leverage Trello for sprint planning, bug tracking, and software release management.

- **Event Planning**: Whether organizing a wedding, conference, or vacation, Trello helps users plan every detail.

- **Personal Productivity**: Individuals use Trello to manage daily tasks, grocery lists, study schedules, and more.

A Brief History of Trello

Trello was created by Fog Creek Software in 2011 as a tool to help manage and visualize project workflows. Its simplicity and effectiveness quickly made it popular, leading to its independence as a separate company, Trello Inc., in 2014. In 2017, **Atlassian**, a global software company known for products like Jira and Confluence, acquired Trello for $425 million, further expanding its capabilities and integrations. Today, Trello continues to evolve, adding new features such as automation, Power-Ups, and advanced team management tools.

Common Myths About Trello

Despite its popularity, there are a few misconceptions about Trello that are worth addressing:

- **"Trello is only for big projects."**
  While Trello is great for large-scale project management, it is equally useful for personal organization and small tasks.

- **"Trello is too simple for professional use."**
  Trello's simplicity is one of its biggest strengths, but its features can be extended with Power-Ups and integrations to handle complex workflows.

- **"You need to pay to use Trello effectively."**
  Trello offers a generous free plan that includes all the essential features needed for task management. Paid plans provide additional functionalities, but many users find the free version sufficient.

Final Thoughts

Trello is an exceptional tool for managing tasks and projects, offering a simple yet powerful approach to organization. Its visual layout, ease of use, and flexibility make it a go-to solution for individuals and teams looking to improve productivity.

In the following sections of this book, we will explore Trello's features in detail, guiding you through the process of setting up your first board, customizing workflows, collaborating with teams, and leveraging automation to boost efficiency. Whether you are a beginner or an experienced user looking to refine your skills, this guide will help you **master task management with ease**.

1.2 Key Benefits of Using Trello

TRELLO 101

Your productivity powerhouse

Stay organized and efficient with Inbox, Boards, and Planner. Every to-do, idea, or responsibility—no matter how small—finds its place, keeping you at the top of your game.

COMING SOON

Inbox

When it's on your mind, it goes in your Inbox. Capture your to-dos from anywhere, anytime.

Boards

Your to-do list may be long, but it can be manageable! Keep tabs on everything from "to-dos to tackle" to "mission accomplished!"

COMING SOON

Planner

Drag, drop, get it done. Snap your top tasks into your calendar and make time for what truly matters.

Trello has become one of the most popular task management and collaboration tools due to its simplicity, flexibility, and effectiveness in organizing work. Whether you're an individual looking to improve personal productivity, a small team managing projects, or a large enterprise coordinating complex workflows, Trello offers a wide range of benefits.

In this section, we will explore the key advantages of using Trello, including its intuitive interface, seamless collaboration, customizability, integration with other tools, automation features, accessibility, and cost-effectiveness.

Intuitive and Easy-to-Use Interface

One of Trello's biggest strengths is its user-friendly and visually appealing interface. Unlike complex project management tools that require extensive training, Trello follows a simple drag-and-drop model that makes it easy to learn and use.

- **Kanban-style layout**: Trello uses the Kanban board system, which organizes tasks into lists and cards, making it visually clear where tasks stand in a workflow.

- **Minimal learning curve**: Even beginners can start using Trello immediately without formal training.

- **Quick setup**: Users can create a new board and start organizing their work within minutes.

- **Real-time updates**: Any changes made to cards, lists, or boards are instantly visible to all users, ensuring smooth communication.

With this **intuitive** and **interactive** design, Trello is an excellent choice for users of all skill levels.

Seamless Collaboration for Teams

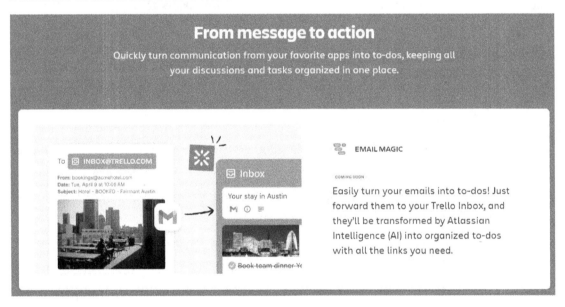

Trello is built with collaboration in mind, allowing teams to work together efficiently regardless of their location. It enhances team communication, transparency, and accountability.

- **Real-time task tracking**: Every team member can see the status of a task at a glance.

- **Assigning tasks**: You can assign members to specific Trello cards so everyone knows who is responsible for what.

- **Commenting and discussions**: Users can leave comments, tag team members, and discuss tasks directly on Trello cards.

- **File sharing**: Attach documents, images, and links directly to cards for easy access.

- **Activity history**: Trello keeps track of all actions taken on a card, ensuring transparency.

This makes Trello perfect for remote teams, freelancers, and businesses of all sizes that need an efficient way to coordinate projects.

Customization and Flexibility

One of Trello's greatest strengths is its flexibility, allowing users to adapt the platform to their specific needs.

- **Custom workflows**: Trello can be used for task management, project planning, content scheduling, CRM, event planning, and more.

- **Custom labels and tags**: Organize tasks by adding colored labels to represent priorities, categories, or progress levels.

- **Personalized board backgrounds**: Change the board's appearance to suit your team's preferences.

- **Checklists and due dates**: Break down large tasks into smaller subtasks and set deadlines for each.

Since Trello is not limited to a single workflow structure, users can build a system that works best for them.

Powerful Integrations with Other Tools

Trello seamlessly integrates with a variety of other apps and services to enhance productivity and streamline workflows. Some key integrations include:

- **Google Drive & Dropbox**: Attach documents and files directly from cloud storage.

- **Slack**: Get Trello notifications in Slack to keep teams updated.

- **Microsoft Teams**: Integrate Trello boards into Microsoft Teams for better collaboration.

- **Zapier & IFTTT**: Automate workflows by connecting Trello with thousands of apps.

- **Jira, Confluence, and GitHub**: Perfect for software development teams.

These integrations eliminate the need to switch between apps constantly, helping teams work more efficiently.

Automation with Butler

Trello's built-in automation tool, Butler, allows users to automate repetitive tasks and save time.

- **Automate card movements**: Move cards to different lists based on due dates or completed checklists.

- **Create custom rules**: Set triggers for notifications, assignments, or actions based on card updates.

- **Recurring tasks**: Automate repetitive tasks such as weekly meetings or monthly reports.

- **Button actions**: Create custom buttons to perform multiple actions with a single click.

With Butler, teams can focus on important work instead of spending time on manual updates.

Accessibility Across Devices

Trello is available on multiple platforms, making it easy to access your projects anytime, anywhere.

- **Web-based**: Use Trello from any browser without downloading software.

- **Mobile apps**: Available for iOS and Android, so you can manage tasks on the go.

- **Desktop apps**: Available for Windows and Mac for enhanced performance.

- **Offline mode**: Work without an internet connection, and Trello will sync changes once you're online.

This makes Trello ideal for teams working remotely or individuals who need constant access to their tasks.

Cost-Effectiveness and Scalability

Trello offers a free plan that is powerful enough for individuals and small teams, making it an excellent option for startups, freelancers, and personal use.

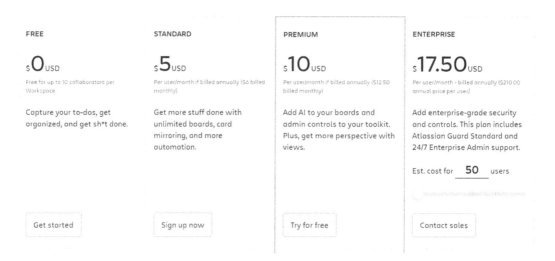

Trello Plans:

- **Free Plan**: Suitable for individuals and small teams with unlimited cards and basic features.

- **Trello Standard**: Adds features like larger file attachments and advanced checklists.

- **Trello Premium**: Ideal for businesses, offering custom views, timelines, and advanced reporting.

- **Trello Enterprise**: Designed for large organizations with enhanced security and administration.

Since Trello is scalable, businesses can start with the free plan and upgrade as their needs grow.

Summary: Why Choose Trello?

To summarize, Trello provides a powerful yet simple way to organize tasks, collaborate with teams, and boost productivity.

✓ **Easy to use** – No technical knowledge required.

✓ **Enhances team collaboration** – Assign tasks, comment, and share files easily.

✓ **Highly customizable** – Adapt Trello to your workflow.

✓ **Integrates with essential tools** – Google Drive, Slack, Jira, and more.

✓ **Automates workflows** – Use Butler to handle repetitive tasks.

✓ **Accessible anywhere** – Web, mobile, and desktop apps.

✓ **Cost-effective** – Start for free and upgrade when needed.

Trello empowers individuals and teams to stay organized, work efficiently, and achieve goals with minimum effort.

In the next section, we will walk you through how to set up your Trello account and get started with your first Trello board. 🚀

Final Thoughts

This section covered the key benefits of using Trello and why it is one of the best task management tools available today. Now that you understand Trello's strengths, you're ready to move forward and start using it effectively in your daily work.

Let's move on to the next section: Setting Up Your Trello Account!

1.3 Setting Up Your Trello Account

Trello is a powerful yet user-friendly tool that allows individuals and teams to manage tasks and projects efficiently. Before you can start organizing your workflow with Trello, the first step is to create and set up your account. This section will guide you through the process of signing up, understanding account settings, and customizing your profile for a seamless Trello experience.

Signing Up for a Trello Account

Creating a Trello account is a quick and straightforward process. Since Trello is a cloud-based platform, you only need an internet connection and a web browser to get started. Follow these steps to sign up:

Step 1: Visit Trello's Website

- Open your preferred web browser and go to www.trello.com.

- Click the **Sign Up** button, usually located in the top-right corner of the page.

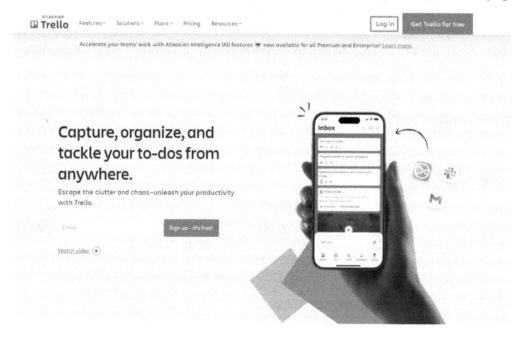

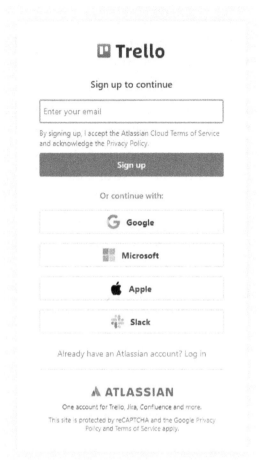

Step 2: Choose a Signup Method

Trello offers multiple ways to sign up for an account:

- **Using an email address**: Enter your email, create a password, and follow the instructions.

- **Signing up with Google**: If you have a Google account, you can sign up with a single click.

- **Signing up with Microsoft or Apple**: Trello allows authentication through Microsoft and Apple accounts for added convenience.

After selecting your preferred method, complete the verification process, which may include confirming your email.

Step 3: Setting Up Your Profile

Once you've signed up, you'll be redirected to the Trello dashboard. Before you start using Trello, take a moment to personalize your account:

- **Add a profile picture**: Click on your avatar in the top-right corner and upload an image.

- **Set your display name**: You can choose a professional name for business use or a nickname for personal projects.

- **Adjust language and timezone settings**: Ensure Trello displays the correct time and language based on your location.

By completing these initial setup steps, you'll be ready to start exploring Trello's features.

Understanding Trello's Account Settings

After signing up, it's important to familiarize yourself with Trello's account settings, which allow you to manage your personal preferences, security settings, and notifications.

Accessing Account Settings

- Click on your profile icon in the top-right corner of the Trello dashboard.

- Select "Settings" from the dropdown menu.

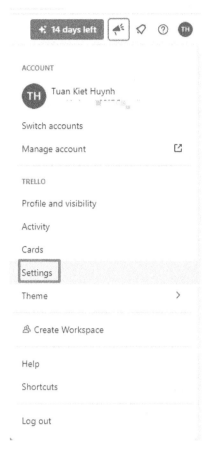

Key Settings to Configure

1. Security and Privacy

- **Change your password**: If you signed up with an email and password, you can update it under the security section.

- **Enable two-factor authentication (2FA)**: Trello offers 2FA for added security, requiring an extra verification step when logging in.

Sessions

If you need to, you can log out of one or all of your other devices.

Manage your recent devices

Two-step verification

Keep your account extra secure with a second login step. Learn more

Configure two-step verification

2. Notifications

- Trello sends notifications for important activities such as task updates, mentions, and due date reminders.

- You can customize how you receive notifications:

  o Email notifications: Receive alerts directly in your inbox.

  o Push notifications: If using Trello's mobile app, enable push notifications for real-time updates.

  o Web notifications: Trello can notify you through browser pop-ups.

3. Connected Apps and Integrations

- Trello allows you to link your account to Google Drive, Slack, Microsoft Teams, and other third-party apps.

- You can manage active integrations in the settings menu to enhance your workflow.

Understanding these settings ensures you have full control over your Trello experience.

Choosing a Trello Plan

Trello offers different plans, ranging from a free version for individuals to enterprise-level solutions for large organizations. Choosing the right plan depends on your needs.

Overview of Trello Plans

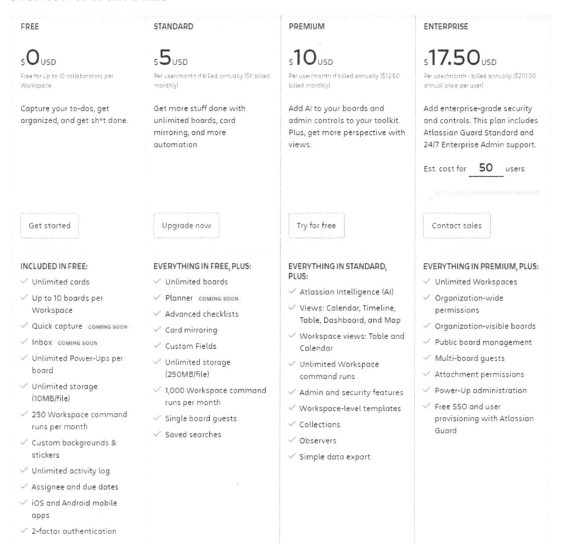

FREE	STANDARD	PREMIUM	ENTERPRISE
$0 USD	$5 USD	$10 USD	$17.50 USD
Free for up to 10 collaborators per Workspace	Per user/month if billed annually ($6 billed monthly)	Per user/month if billed annually ($12.50 billed monthly)	Per user/month - billed annually ($210.00 annual price per user)
Capture your to-dos, get organized, and get sh*t done.	Get more stuff done with unlimited boards, card mirroring, and more automation.	Add AI to your boards and admin controls to your toolkit. Plus, get more perspective with views.	Add enterprise-grade security and controls. This plan includes Atlassian Guard Standard and 24/7 Enterprise Admin support.
			Est. cost for **50** users
Get started	Upgrade now	Try for free	Contact sales
INCLUDED IN FREE:	**EVERYTHING IN FREE, PLUS:**	**EVERYTHING IN STANDARD, PLUS:**	**EVERYTHING IN PREMIUM, PLUS:**
✓ Unlimited cards	✓ Unlimited boards	✓ Atlassian Intelligence (AI)	✓ Unlimited Workspaces
✓ Up to 10 boards per Workspace	✓ Planner COMING SOON	✓ Views: Calendar, Timeline, Table, Dashboard, and Map	✓ Organization-wide permissions
✓ Quick capture COMING SOON	✓ Advanced checklists	✓ Workspace views: Table and Calendar	✓ Organization-visible boards
✓ Inbox COMING SOON	✓ Card mirroring	✓ Unlimited Workspace command runs	✓ Public board management
✓ Unlimited Power-Ups per board	✓ Custom Fields	✓ Admin and security features	✓ Multi-board guests
✓ Unlimited storage (10MB/file)	✓ Unlimited storage (250MB/file)	✓ Workspace-level templates	✓ Attachment permissions
✓ 250 Workspace command runs per month	✓ 1,000 Workspace command runs per month	✓ Collections	✓ Power-Up administration
✓ Custom backgrounds & stickers	✓ Single board guests	✓ Observers	✓ Free SSO and user provisioning with Atlassian Guard
✓ Unlimited activity log	✓ Saved searches	✓ Simple data export	
✓ Assignee and due dates			
✓ iOS and Android mobile apps			
✓ 2-factor authentication			

How to Upgrade Your Plan

- Go to **Settings** > **Billing**.

- Select the plan that fits your needs and follow the payment instructions.

If you're new to Trello, the Free Plan is a great starting point, and you can upgrade later as needed.

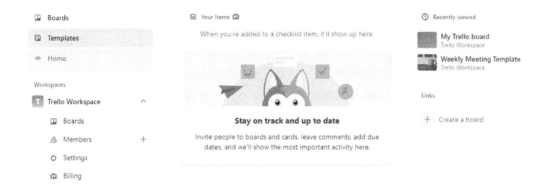

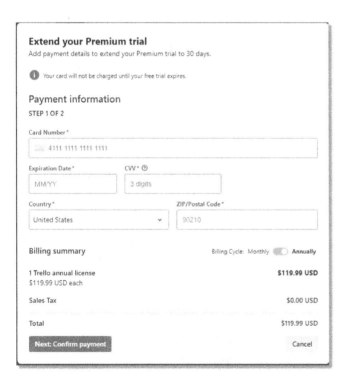

Installing Trello on Different Devices

Trello is available across multiple platforms, making it easy to access your tasks from anywhere.

1. Web-Based Trello

- Trello works directly in your web browser, so there's no need to install anything.

- Compatible with Chrome, Firefox, Safari, and Edge.

2. Desktop Applications

- Trello offers dedicated apps for Windows and Mac.

- Download from www.trello.com/download.

3. Mobile Applications

- iOS (App Store) and Android (Google Play Store) versions are available.

- Features include push notifications, offline access, and quick task updates.

By installing Trello on your preferred devices, you ensure seamless access to your projects anytime, anywhere.

Summary: Getting Started with Trello

By now, you should have a fully functional Trello account and be ready to explore the platform. Let's recap the key steps:

✓ Sign up for an account using email, Google, Microsoft, or Apple.
✓ Customize account settings to improve security and user experience.
✓ Choose the right Trello plan based on your needs.
✓ Install Trello on multiple devices for seamless access.
✓ Set up and personalize your first board for effective task management.

In the next section, we will dive into Trello's core features, including boards, lists, and cards, and how to use them effectively for project management.

1.4 Navigating the Trello Interface

1.4.1 The Trello Dashboard

The **Trello Dashboard** is the central hub where users can manage boards, navigate between workspaces, and access essential settings. Whether you're working alone or collaborating with a team, understanding how to navigate the Trello Dashboard efficiently will help you organize tasks, streamline workflows, and maximize productivity.

This section will guide you through the key components of the Trello Dashboard, including how to access boards, use workspaces, manage notifications, and customize the dashboard to suit your needs.

Overview of the Trello Dashboard

When you log into Trello, the first screen you see is the **Trello Dashboard**. It provides a **bird's-eye view** of all your boards and workspaces, allowing you to quickly jump into projects or manage tasks.

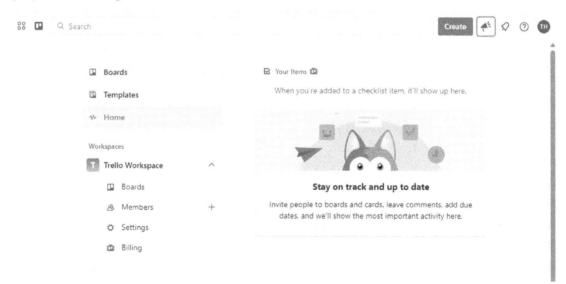

The Trello Dashboard consists of several key elements:

1. **Navigation Bar** – The top bar where you can search for boards, access notifications, and modify settings.

2. **Workspaces Panel** – Displays all your workspaces and allows quick navigation between them.

3. **Boards Section** – Shows recent boards, starred boards, and workspace-specific boards.

4. **Create Button** – A shortcut for quickly creating new boards, lists, or cards.

5. **Notifications & Activity Feed** – Alerts you to updates, mentions, and task changes.

6. **User Profile & Settings** – Customize Trello to fit your workflow preferences.

Let's explore each of these elements in detail.

Navigating the Navigation Bar

At the top of the Trello Dashboard, you'll find the **Navigation Bar**, which provides quick access to core Trello functions.

Key Features in the Navigation Bar:

🔍 **Search Bar** – Quickly find specific boards, lists, or cards using keywords.

📌 **Starred Boards** – View and access boards that you have marked as important.

🔔 **Notifications Icon** – See real-time updates on mentions, due dates, and comments.

⚙️ **Settings Menu** – Adjust user preferences, integrations, and workspace settings.

➕ **Create Button** – Instantly add a new board, list, or card without navigating away.

The **Search Bar** is particularly useful when working with multiple boards, allowing you to locate tasks or projects quickly.

Understanding Workspaces and Boards

Trello organizes tasks using a hierarchical structure:

📁 **Workspaces** → 📋 **Boards** → 🗒 **Lists** → ✅ **Cards**

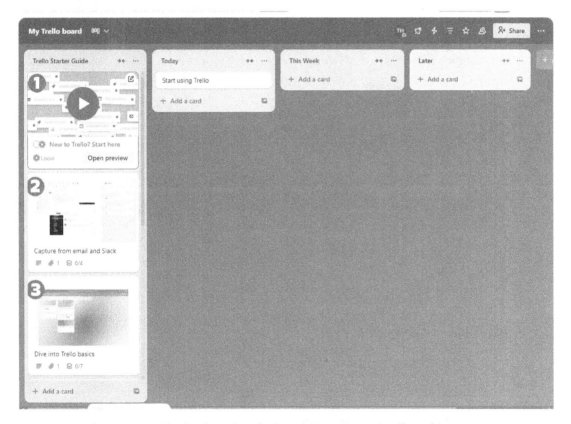

- **Workspaces** – The highest level of organization in Trello, where teams can group related boards together.

- **Boards** – Individual project spaces where tasks are managed using lists and cards.

- **Lists** – Containers within boards that help structure tasks (e.g., To-Do, In Progress, Done).

- **Cards** – Individual tasks or action items within lists.

You can access different workspaces and boards from the Trello Dashboard's left sidebar, making it easy to switch between projects.

Managing Boards from the Dashboard

The Boards Section of the Dashboard allows you to access and manage your boards efficiently. It includes:

📌 **Starred Boards** – Boards you frequently use, pinned for quick access.
📅 **Recent Boards** – Displays boards you have recently worked on.
🗂 **Workspace Boards** – Lists all boards within a selected workspace.

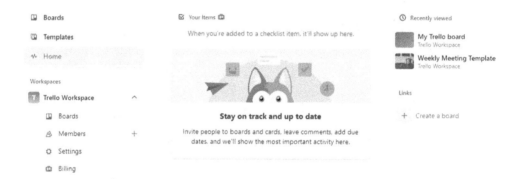

How to Star a Board for Quick Access:

1. Open the board you frequently use.

2. Click on the **three-dot menu** at the top right.

3. Select **"Star this board"** to pin it for easy access.

This feature is particularly useful for users managing multiple projects at once.

Notifications and Activity Feed

The Notifications and Activity Feed keeps you informed about updates and changes within your Trello boards.

🔔 **Notifications**:

- Displays mentions, comments, and due date reminders.
- Accessible via the **bell icon** in the top navigation bar.
- Can be customized to receive only critical updates.

🔊 **Activity Feed**:

- Shows a real-time log of all actions taken on a board.
- Allows team members to track changes and updates easily.

How to Manage Notifications:

1. Click the **bell icon** in the top right corner.
2. Review recent notifications.
3. Click on any notification to navigate directly to the related task.
4. Adjust notification preferences in **Settings** to avoid unnecessary alerts.

Managing notifications effectively helps users stay on top of important updates without feeling overwhelmed.

Customizing Your Trello Dashboard

Trello allows users to customize the Dashboard for a personalized experience.

🎨 **Change Board Backgrounds** – Add colors, patterns, or images to differentiate projects.

📁 **Organize Boards by Category** – Use workspaces to group related boards together.

⚡ **Enable Dark Mode** – Reduce eye strain for better productivity.

📌 **Use Power-Ups** – Integrate additional tools like calendar views or automation.

How to Change Your Board Background:

1. Open a board from the Dashboard.

2. Click on **"Show Menu"** on the right.

3. Select **"Change Background"** and choose a color or image.

4. Save changes and return to the Dashboard.

These small customization tweaks can significantly enhance the visual clarity and usability of Trello.

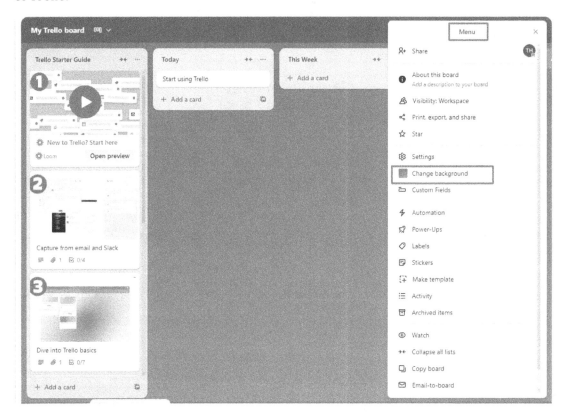

Summary: Mastering the Trello Dashboard

Mastering the Trello Dashboard is essential for efficiently managing boards, accessing workspaces, and tracking notifications. Let's recap the key takeaways:

✓ The Navigation Bar provides quick access to searches, notifications, and settings.
✓ Workspaces and Boards structure your tasks in an intuitive hierarchy.
✓ The Boards Section helps manage recent, starred, and workspace boards.

✅ Notifications and Activity Feed keep you updated on task changes and mentions.

✅ Customization options allow users to personalize the dashboard for better organization.

By understanding and utilizing these features, you'll be able to navigate Trello with confidence, saving time and improving productivity.

Next Steps: Navigating Boards, Lists, and Cards

Now that you're familiar with the Trello Dashboard, the next step is to explore how boards, lists, and cards function. In the following section, we'll dive deeper into:

📌 How to create and manage boards

📋 The role of lists in structuring workflows

👨‍💼 Managing tasks effectively with Trello cards

With this knowledge, you'll be ready to take full control of your projects and tasks using Trello. Let's continue! 🚀

1.4.2 Boards, Lists, and Cards Overview

Trello's Boards, Lists, and Cards form the foundation of its task management system. Understanding how these elements work together will help you create an efficient workflow, stay organized, and collaborate seamlessly with your team.

In this section, we will explore the purpose of each component, how they interact, and best practices for using them effectively.

What Are Boards, Lists, and Cards?

Trello is based on the Kanban methodology, a visual system that helps users track progress through different stages. Trello implements this using three core elements:

- **Boards**: Represent the overall project or workspace.

- **Lists**: Organize tasks within a board into stages or categories.

- **Cards**: Represent individual tasks, ideas, or pieces of work.

Each of these components plays a crucial role in managing projects, tracking progress, and improving productivity.

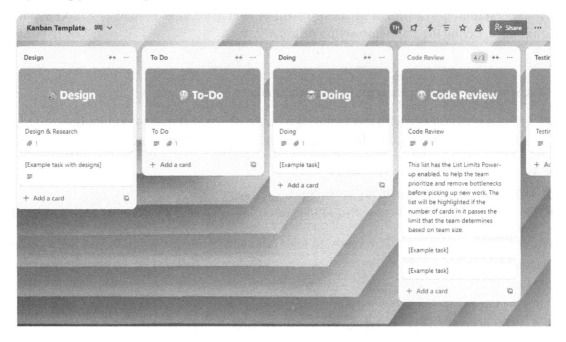

Trello Boards: The Big Picture

What is a Trello Board?

A board in Trello represents a project, workflow, or workspace. It acts as the main dashboard where tasks are organized and tracked. Each board consists of lists and cards that provide structure to your work.

For example:

- A **Marketing Team** can have a board for managing **content planning**.

- A **Software Development Team** can use a board for **tracking bug fixes**.

- A **Student** can use a board for **managing assignments and deadlines**.

Creating a Board

To create a board:

1. Click the **"Create new board"** button on the Trello homepage.

2. Enter a **board name** (e.g., "Product Launch Plan").

3. Choose a **visibility setting** (Private, Workspace, or Public).

4. Select a **background theme** to customize its appearance.

5. Click **"Create Board"** to start organizing tasks.

Customizing a Board

Once your board is set up, you can personalize it:

✅ **Rename the board** to reflect your project.
✅ **Set a background image** for visual appeal.
✅ **Enable power-ups** (e.g., Calendar, Custom Fields).
✅ **Add team members** for collaboration.

A well-organized board provides a **clear overview of your project**, ensuring that all tasks are properly categorized.

Trello Lists: Structuring Your Workflow

What is a Trello List?

A list in Trello organizes tasks into stages of a workflow. Lists are placed horizontally across the board and can represent statuses, priorities, or categories.

For example:

- A Content Creation Board might have:

    o 📝 To Write

    o 🔄 In Progress

- ○ ✓ Published

- A Project Management Board might include:

  - ○ ☐ Backlog

  - ○ 𝕪 In Development

  - ○ 🚀 Completed

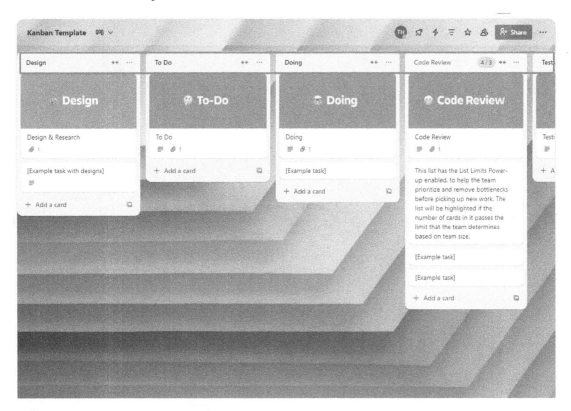

Creating and Managing Lists

To create a list:

1. Click **"Add a list"** on the Trello board.

2. Type a **list name** (e.g., "To-Do").

3. Press **Enter** to add it.

To **rearrange lists**, simply **drag and drop** them to the desired position. You can also:

✅ **Move lists** between boards.

✅ **Copy lists** to duplicate workflows.

✅ **Archive lists** to remove them from view without deleting data.

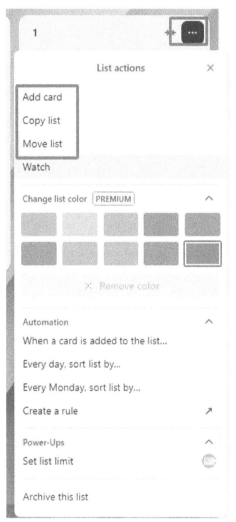

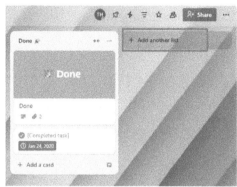

Common List Structures

Here are some best practice list structures for different use cases:

1. Simple To-Do System

✅ To-Do → ☐ In Progress → ✅ Done

2. Agile Development Board

📌 Backlog → 🚀 Sprint Planning → 🏹 In Progress → 🏁 Completed

3. Sales Pipeline

📞 Leads → ✉ Contacted → 💰 Negotiation → ✅ Closed

By structuring lists properly, you ensure that your workflow is **clear and easy to track**.

Trello Cards: Managing Tasks and Details

What is a Trello Card?

A **card** in Trello represents an **individual task, idea, or item**. It holds detailed information, including:

- Task descriptions
- Assigned members
- Due dates
- Checklists
- Attachments
- Comments

Creating and Editing Cards

To create a card:

1. Click **"Add a card"** at the bottom of a list.

2. Enter a **card title** (e.g., "Write Blog Post").

3. Click **"Add Card"** to save it.

To edit a card:

✓ Click the card to open its **detailed view**.

✓ Modify the **title, description, or labels**.

✓ Assign it to a **team member**.

✓ Set a **due date** to track deadlines.

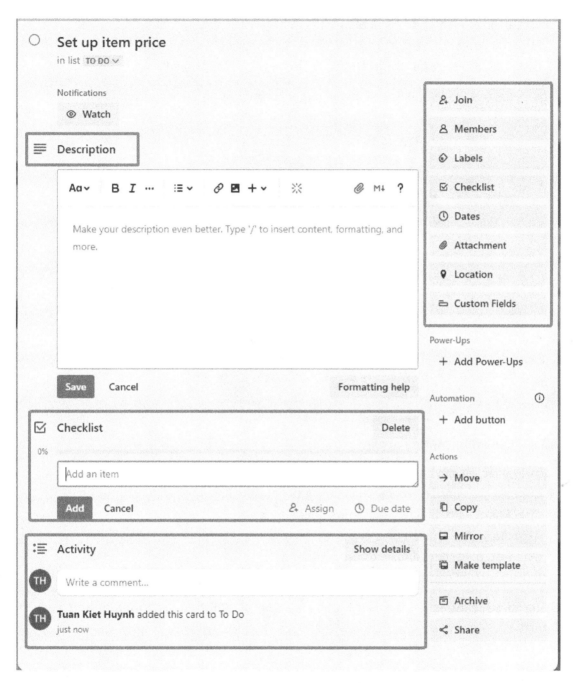

Moving Cards Between Lists

Cards can be moved between lists to reflect progress:

🖊 Move "Write Blog Post" from "To-Do" → "In Progress" → "Published".

🎯 Drag "Client Proposal" from "Draft" → "Review" → "Approved".

This visual workflow makes task management effortless and transparent.

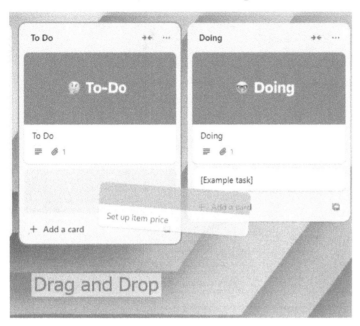

Additional Features on Cards

Each Trello card can be **customized** to suit your needs:

✓ **Labels** – Categorize tasks with color-coded tags.

✓ **Checklists** – Break down tasks into smaller steps.

✓ **Attachments** – Upload files, links, or images.

✓ **Due Dates** – Set deadlines for accountability.

✓ **Comments** – Communicate with team members.

Using these features helps ensure that each task is **detailed, actionable, and easy to follow**.

Best Practices for Using Boards, Lists, and Cards

1. Keep Boards Organized

✓ Limit the number of lists to avoid clutter.

✓ Use **clear names** for boards and lists.

✓ Regularly **archive old cards** to maintain clarity.

2. Use Lists to Represent Workflow Stages

✓ Design a **logical flow** from left to right.

✓ Avoid too many **"In Progress"** tasks to prevent overload.

✓ Use **Backlog** lists to store low-priority tasks.

3. Make Cards Actionable

✓ Write **clear and concise** card titles.

✓ Use **checklists** to break down complex tasks.

✓ Assign cards to team members for accountability.

Summary: How Boards, Lists, and Cards Work Together

Trello's **Boards, Lists, and Cards** provide a **simple yet powerful system** for managing tasks effectively:

- Boards represent projects.

- Lists organize tasks into stages.

- Cards contain task details and updates.

By understanding how these elements function together, you can build an organized and efficient workflow for any project.

Next Steps

Now that you understand Boards, Lists, and Cards, the next section will explore Trello Navigation and Settings, where we will dive deeper into customizing your experience.

📌 **Next up: 1.4.3 Trello Navigation and Settings!** 🚀

1.4.3 Trello Navigation and Settings

Trello is known for its intuitive and user-friendly interface, which makes it easy for both beginners and experienced users to navigate. To maximize efficiency and streamline workflow, it's essential to understand how to move around Trello's interface and customize its settings.

In this section, we will explore Trello's main navigation elements, settings options, and ways to optimize your user experience. By mastering these aspects, you will be able to tailor Trello to suit your needs and work more efficiently.

Understanding Trello's Navigation Elements

Trello's navigation system is designed to provide quick access to all essential features while maintaining a clean and clutter-free interface. The key navigation elements include:

A. The Header Bar

At the top of every Trello page, you will find the header bar, which contains several important navigation tools:

- **Trello Home Button**: Clicking the Trello logo takes you back to the home screen, where you can access all your boards.

- **Search Bar**: Allows you to quickly find boards, cards, members, or specific content within Trello.

- **Create Button (+ Icon)**: Lets you create new boards, cards, workspaces, or templates instantly.

- **Notifications Bell**: Displays real-time updates about mentions, changes to your cards, or team activity.

- **User Profile & Settings**: Located on the far right, this gives you access to account settings, preferences, and Trello help resources.

B. The Sidebar Menu

Trello's **left-hand sidebar** provides access to all your **boards and workspaces**:

- **Home**: The dashboard that displays your **recently accessed boards**, notifications, and workspace overviews.

- **Workspaces**: A list of all your workspaces and boards for quick switching.

- **Boards**: Displays all Trello boards you have access to within your selected workspace.

- **Templates**: Browse pre-made Trello templates to get started faster.

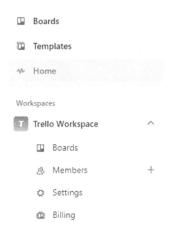

C. The Board View

Once inside a Trello board, you will see its **core navigation elements**, including:

- **Board Title**: Located at the top left, showing the name of the board.

- **Board Menu (Right Sidebar)**: Contains board settings, filters, activity logs, and automation tools.

- **Lists and Cards**: The main workspace where tasks are organized visually.

- **Add List and Add Card Buttons**: Allows you to create new lists and tasks effortlessly.

By familiarizing yourself with these **essential navigation elements**, you can efficiently move between boards, find information quickly, and optimize your workflow.

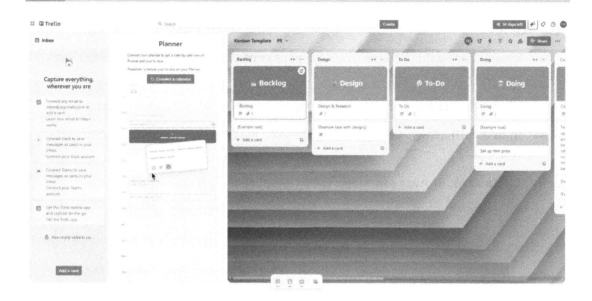

Customizing Trello Settings for Better Workflow

Trello offers a range of customization options that allow users to personalize their experience. The settings menu can be accessed through the user profile icon in the top right corner. Let's explore some key customization options:

A. Personal Account Settings

Under the Account Settings section, users can:

- Change their name and profile picture to personalize their account.

- Update their email address and password for security.

- Enable two-factor authentication (2FA) for enhanced protection.

- Manage notifications to control email and in-app alerts.

- Change language and timezone for localization preferences.

B. Board and Workspace Settings

Each Trello board and workspace has its own settings that users can configure.

1. **Board Settings**:
   - Change board visibility (Private, Workspace-visible, or Public).

- Rename the board title.
- Enable or disable comments from non-members.
- Set custom backgrounds for personalization.
- Enable or disable the card aging feature to track inactive cards.

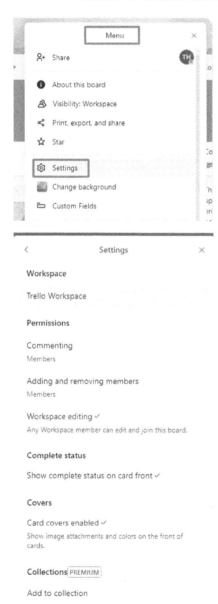

2. **Workspace Settings**:
   - Add or remove team members.
   - Adjust permission levels (Admin, Normal, Observer).
   - Upgrade to Trello Premium or Enterprise for advanced features.

C. Notification Settings

Managing notifications properly helps users stay updated without being overwhelmed. Trello allows you to:

- Receive desktop, email, or mobile notifications for important activity.

- Customize notification frequency (Instant, Periodic, or Weekly Summary).

- Mute specific boards if you don't want alerts from them.

Proper notification management ensures you stay informed without unnecessary distractions.

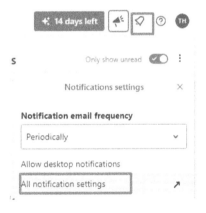

Using Filters and Search for Faster Navigation

Trello provides powerful search and filtering options to help users locate information quickly.

A. Advanced Search in Trello

The search bar, located at the top of the Trello interface, allows you to find:

- Cards by title, labels, or keywords.

- Boards you have access to.

- Members assigned to tasks.

For more precise results, Trello supports search operators such as:

- label:urgent → Finds all cards with the "urgent" label.

- due:overdue → Displays overdue tasks.

- @me → Shows all cards assigned to you.

B. Using Board Filters

If you have a large board, filters help narrow down information:

- Filter by labels to view only tasks with specific categories.

- Filter by members to see who is assigned to what.

- Filter by due dates to prioritize upcoming deadlines.

Using search and filters efficiently makes navigating Trello much faster and more convenient.

Advanced Trello Navigation Tips and Shortcuts

To boost productivity, Trello offers keyboard shortcuts and navigation tips:

A. Essential Keyboard Shortcuts

- B → Open Board Menu for quick board switching.

- F → Open Filter Cards menu.

- Q → Show only your assigned cards.

- D → Open Due Date Picker for selected cards.

- C → Archive a card.

- Spacebar → Assign/unassign yourself from a card.

- E → Edit card title instantly.

B. Quick Navigation Tips

- Drag and drop cards between lists to update status.

- Use the "Watch" feature to get updates on specific cards.

- Pin important boards to access them quickly from the sidebar.

- Use Butler Automation to set up auto-moves and reminders.

By mastering these shortcuts and tricks, you can navigate Trello faster and more efficiently.

Summary: Mastering Trello Navigation and Settings

Understanding Trello's navigation and settings allows users to work more efficiently and customize their experience. Here's a recap of what we covered:

✓ Main navigation elements: Header bar, sidebar menu, and board view.
✓ Customizing account and board settings: Personalization, security, and permissions.
✓ Using filters and search tools: Finding tasks faster with keywords and labels.
✓ Boosting productivity with shortcuts: Quick commands for smooth navigation.

By applying these best practices, you will navigate Trello effortlessly and optimize it for maximum productivity.

Next Steps

Now that you're comfortable with Trello's interface and settings, the next step is to explore Trello's core features, starting with boards, lists, and cards. In the next chapter, we'll dive deeper into how to create, manage, and customize your Trello boards for better organization. 🖋

CHAPTER II
Understanding Trello's Core Features

2.1 Boards: Organizing Your Workspaces

2.1.1 Creating a New Board

Trello's board-based structure is one of its defining features, making it an excellent tool for organizing tasks, projects, and workflows. A Trello board serves as a visual workspace where you can manage tasks, track progress, and collaborate with team members.

In this section, we will explore the process of creating a new board in Trello, covering:

- The importance of boards in Trello

- Step-by-step instructions to create a new board

- Customization options for better organization

- Best practices for structuring boards efficiently

By the end of this section, you will have a fully functional Trello board tailored to your needs.

Understanding the Role of a Trello Board

A Trello board represents a project, workflow, or workspace where tasks are visually organized. Each board consists of lists (which define stages of work) and cards (which represent individual tasks).

Here are some common use cases for Trello boards:

✅ **Project management** – Track progress of tasks in a structured workflow

✅ **Task organization** – Plan daily, weekly, or long-term goals

✅ **Team collaboration** – Assign tasks and communicate with colleagues

✅ **Content planning** – Manage editorial calendars for blogs, social media, etc.

✅ **Event planning** – Coordinate logistics for personal or business events

Regardless of the purpose, Trello boards provide a flexible and intuitive way to keep work organized and accessible.

Step-by-Step Guide to Creating a New Trello Board

Creating a new board in Trello is quick and straightforward. Follow these steps to get started:

Step 1: Log in to Your Trello Account

- Visit trello.com and log in with your Google account, Microsoft account, or email and password.

- If you don't have an account yet, sign up for free.

Step 2: Click "Create New Board"

- From the Trello homepage, locate the **"Create new board"** option.

- You may see this button under:

   o   The **Boards** section on the homepage

   o   The **+ (plus sign)** on the top-right corner of the screen

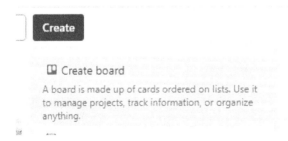

Step 3: Name Your Board

- Enter a clear and descriptive name for your board.

- Examples:

    o ☑ Marketing Campaign 2025 (for marketing teams)

    o ☑ Software Development Sprint (for agile teams)

    o ☑ Personal Productivity Board (for self-organization)

Step 4: Choose a Background

- Trello allows you to customize your board's appearance by selecting:

- o   Solid colors for a simple layout

- o   Custom images to make it visually appealing

◆ *Tip:* Pick a background that suits the theme of your project to enhance clarity and focus.

Step 5: Select Your Workspace

- If you are part of multiple teams or workspaces, choose where the board should belong.

- If you are using Trello individually, select **"Personal Boards"**.

Step 6: Set Board Visibility

- Trello offers **visibility options**:

  - o   **Private** – Only invited members can see it (best for personal tasks).

  - o   **Workspace** – Only members of a specific workspace can view and edit.

  - o   **Public** – Anyone with the link can see it (useful for community boards).

◆ *Tip:* Keep sensitive information private and set appropriate permissions for team collaboration.

Step 7: Click "Create"

- Once all details are set, click **"Create Board"** to finalize your setup.

🎉 **Congratulations!** You have successfully created your Trello board.

Customizing Your Trello Board

Once your board is set up, you can personalize it further for better usability.

Adding Lists to Structure Your Workflow

- Lists help categorize tasks and define the flow of work.

- Common list structures include:

  - o   To-Do / In Progress / Done (Simple task tracking)

  - o   Backlog / Sprint / Review / Completed (Agile development) o   Ideas / Writing / Editing / Published (Content creation)

♦ *Tip:* Name lists according to your specific workflow for clarity.

Enabling Power-Ups for Extra Functionality

Trello allows users to enhance their boards with Power-Ups, which are integrations with other tools.

- Examples of useful Power-Ups:
    - Calendar View – See due dates in a calendar format
    - Google Drive – Attach documents directly to Trello cards
    - Butler Automation – Automate repetitive actions

♦ *Tip:* Choose Power-Ups based on your workflow to avoid unnecessary complexity.

Setting Up Labels for Organization

- Labels help categorize and prioritize tasks.
- Example color codes:
    - ● Urgent – Needs immediate attention
    - ☐ Completed – Successfully finished tasks
    - ◕ Pending Approval – Awaiting review

♦ *Tip:* Use labels consistently across your board to maintain clarity.

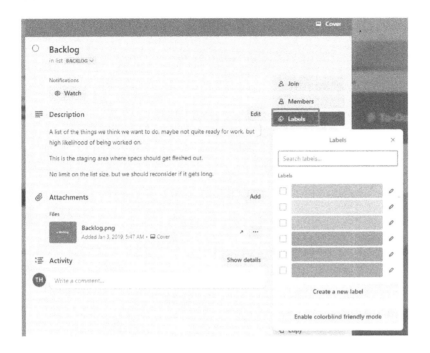

Best Practices for Creating Effective Trello Boards

To make the most of your Trello board, consider the following best practices:

✓ Keep it simple – Avoid clutter; only add essential lists and cards.
✓ Use a consistent naming structure – Helps team members navigate easily.
✓ Regularly update and clean the board – Remove unnecessary cards.
✓ Set due dates and reminders – Keeps tasks on schedule.
✓ Encourage team collaboration – Assign tasks and communicate clearly.

By following these best practices, you can maximize efficiency and productivity in Trello.

Summary: Creating a New Trello Board

To recap, creating a Trello board is a straightforward but important step in setting up an organized workflow. Here's what we covered:

★ Trello boards act as digital workspaces for organizing tasks and projects.
★ Creating a new board involves naming it, setting visibility, and customizing it.

📌 Lists, labels, and Power-Ups enhance board usability.

📌 Best practices ensure an efficient and productive workflow.

With your new Trello board set up, the next step is learning how to structure your lists effectively. In the next section, we'll dive into how lists help organize your workflow and best practices for setting them up. 🚀

Final Thoughts

Creating a Trello board is the foundation of efficient task management. Whether you're using Trello for personal projects, business workflows, or team collaboration, setting up a well-structured board will significantly improve productivity.

Now that you know how to create a board, let's move on to understanding lists in Trello and how they help structure tasks effectively. Let's continue! 🎯

2.1.2 Customizing Board Backgrounds and Settings

One of the best things about Trello is that it allows users to personalize their boards, making them more visually appealing and better suited to specific projects. Customizing board backgrounds and settings not only enhances the user experience but also helps improve workflow organization and team collaboration.

In this section, we will explore the different ways to customize Trello boards, including changing backgrounds, modifying board settings, setting permissions, enabling Power-Ups, and optimizing board views.

Why Customize Your Trello Board?

Before diving into the details of customization, let's first understand why it's important:

✅ **Improves visual organization** – A well-customized board helps users quickly identify tasks, priorities, and workflow stages.

✅ **Enhances team collaboration** – Different teams can create board styles that align with their unique workflow.

✅ **Boosts productivity** – Color-coded boards and organized layouts help users focus on the right tasks.

✅ **Creates a more enjoyable experience** – Personalized boards make task management feel less monotonous.

Now, let's explore how to customize your Trello board.

Changing the Board Background

One of the easiest ways to customize a Trello board is by changing the background. Trello provides several options for backgrounds, including solid colors, high-quality images, and custom uploads (for paid users).

Steps to Change the Background

1. **Open the board** you want to customize.

2. Click on the **"Show Menu"** button in the top right corner.

3. Select **"Change Background."**

4. Choose from the following options:
   - **Colors**: Select a solid color background from Trello's default options.
   - **Photos (Unsplash Integration)**: Choose a high-quality image from Unsplash's free photo library.
   - **Custom Images (Paid Feature)**: Upload your own background image if you have a Trello Premium or Enterprise plan.

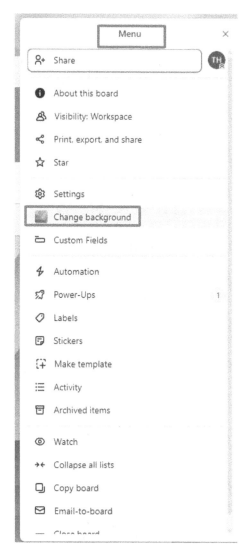

Best Practices for Background Selection

- **Use colors strategically** – Bright colors can be energizing, while muted tones can reduce distractions.

- **Match the theme to your project** – A professional project board might benefit from a clean, simple design, while a creative brainstorming board might use vibrant imagery.

- **Avoid overly busy backgrounds** – Too much detail can make text hard to read.

Customizing Board Settings

Beyond backgrounds, Trello offers several board settings that help fine-tune the functionality of your workspace.

1. Changing Board Name and Description

To rename your board or add a description:

- Click on the **board title** at the top-left corner.

- Type in the new **board name**.

- Click **"Add a Description"** to include important details about the board's purpose.

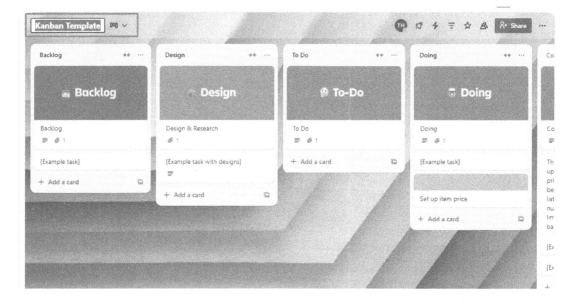

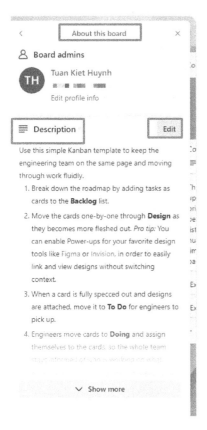

Pro Tip: A clear and concise board name (e.g., "Marketing Campaigns Q3" or "Client Onboarding Tracker") helps users instantly recognize the board's function.

2. Setting Board Visibility and Permissions

Trello offers different visibility settings to control who can access and modify a board.

Visibility Options

- **Private** – Only invited members can view or edit the board. (Best for confidential projects)

- **Workspace Visible** – Anyone in the same Trello workspace can access the board. (Good for team collaboration)

- **Public** – The board is accessible by anyone with the link. (Useful for sharing templates or resources)

Managing Permissions

- **Admin (Owner)** – Full control over the board, including adding/removing members and changing settings.

- **Normal (Member)** – Can edit, move, and delete cards but cannot change board settings.

- **Observer (Read-Only)** – Can view the board but cannot make changes. (Available on paid plans)

To change these settings, click on **"Show Menu"** → **"More"** → **"Settings"** and select the appropriate option.

---

3. Enabling Power-Ups to Enhance Board Functionality

Power-Ups are **add-ons** that expand Trello's features, allowing users to integrate additional tools and automations.

How to Enable Power-Ups

1. Open the board and click on **"Show Menu"**.

2. Select **"Power-Ups"** and browse available options.

3. Click **"Enable"** on any Power-Up you want to use.

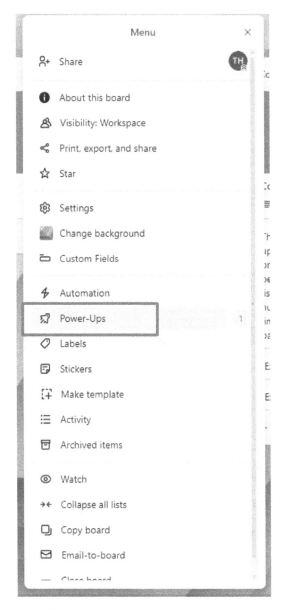

Popular Power-Ups

- **Calendar View** – See due dates in a calendar format.

- **Card Repeater** – Automate recurring tasks.

- **Voting** – Allow team members to vote on tasks.

- **Slack Integration** – Get Trello notifications directly in Slack.

Since free Trello accounts are limited to **one Power-Up per board**, choose carefully!

4. Optimizing Board Views (Premium Feature)

For users with Trello Premium or Enterprise, different board views can enhance productivity:

- **Timeline View** – Helps manage project deadlines.

- **Table View** – Organizes tasks in a structured, spreadsheet-like format.

- **Dashboard View** – Provides insights into productivity trends.

- **Calendar View** – Displays due dates in a monthly layout.

To change board views, go to **"Views"** in the top menu and select the desired option.

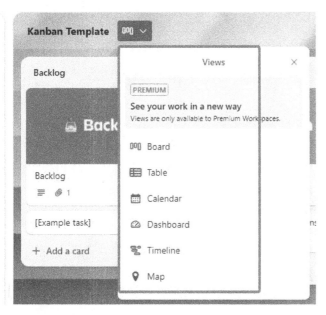

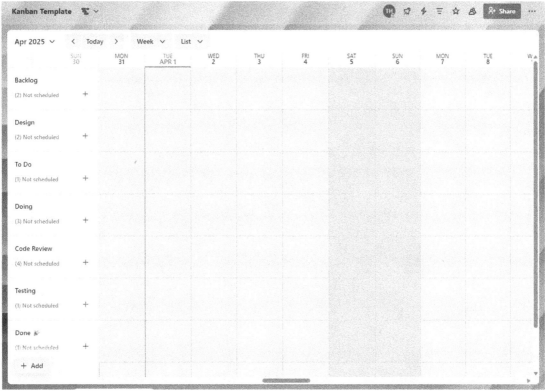

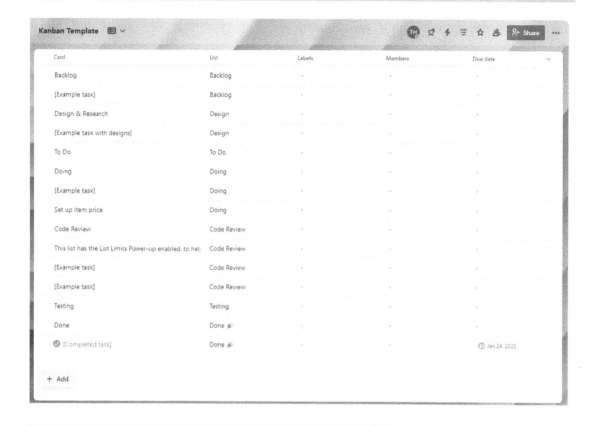

Creating a Cohesive Trello Experience with Customization

A well-customized Trello board should be:

✓ **Visually appealing** – Use colors and images that enhance clarity.

✓ **Efficiently structured** – Name lists and labels clearly for easy navigation.

✓ **Collaborative** – Set appropriate permissions so everyone has the right level of access.

✓ **Enhanced with Power-Ups** – Use integrations to improve productivity.

By following these guidelines, you can ensure that your Trello board is not only functional but also enjoyable to use.

Final Thoughts

Customizing board backgrounds and settings in Trello is a simple yet powerful way to optimize your workflow. Whether you're managing a personal project, a small team, or a large enterprise, personalizing your board will help you stay organized and boost productivity.

In the next section, we'll explore how to structure your workflow effectively using lists and cards, the core building blocks of Trello!

2.2 Lists: Structuring Your Workflow

Trello's list system is one of the core components that help users structure their workflow effectively. Lists are used to categorize tasks, track progress, and organize work within a board. Whether you're managing a personal to-do list, a team project, or a business pipeline, Trello lists provide a flexible way to keep everything organized.

In this section, we'll explore how lists function in Trello, how to create and manage them efficiently, and best practices for structuring your workflow for maximum productivity.

2.2.1 Creating and Managing Lists

Lists in Trello help users break down projects into manageable stages or categories. Each Trello board consists of multiple lists, and within each list, users can create cards that represent specific tasks.

How to Create a List in Trello

Creating a new list in Trello is a simple process. Follow these steps:

1. **Open a Trello board**: Navigate to the board where you want to create a list.

2. **Click on "+ Add a list"**: This option appears on the right side of your existing lists.

3. **Enter a list name**: Choose a descriptive name that represents a stage of your workflow (e.g., "To-Do," "In Progress," "Completed").

4. **Click "Add List"**: Your new list will appear immediately on the board.

You can create **as many lists as needed**, and they can be moved around to better structure your workflow.

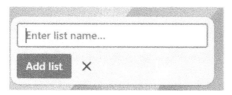

How to Rename a List

If you need to **change the name of a list**, simply:

1. Click on the list title.

2. Type the new name.

3. Press "Enter" to save the changes.

Renaming lists helps **adapt your board** as your project evolves.

How to Move a List

Trello allows users to **rearrange lists** by dragging them to a different position on the board. This flexibility is useful when adjusting workflows based on priorities.

To move a list:

1. Click and hold the list's title.

2. Drag it to the desired location.

3. Release to drop it into place.

You can rearrange lists as often as needed, ensuring your workflow remains optimized.

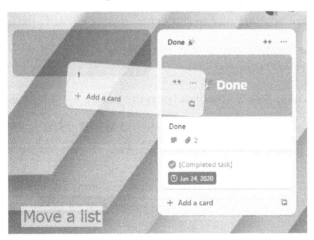

How to Archive or Delete a List

If a list is no longer needed, you have the option to **archive** or **delete** it.

- **Archiving a list**:
  - Click the three dots (menu) at the top of the list.
  - Select "Archive this list."
  - The list will be removed from the board but can be restored later if needed.

- **Deleting a list**:
  - Trello does not allow direct deletion of lists.
  - Instead, archive the list first, then go to the **Archived Items** section and delete it permanently.

Archiving is useful when you **want to keep a record** of completed tasks without cluttering your board.

Best Practices for Managing Lists Effectively

Creating lists is just the beginning. To maximize **efficiency**, consider these best practices when managing lists in Trello.

1. Keep Lists Concise and Focused

- Avoid overloading lists with too many cards, as it can become overwhelming.

- Keep lists specific to stages of a process rather than general categories.

- Example: Instead of "Tasks," use "To-Do", "In Progress", and "Completed" to create a clear workflow.

2. Use Consistent Naming Conventions

- Choose names that clearly indicate their purpose.

- Example: If managing a content calendar, use lists like "Idea Stage," "Writing," "Editing," and "Published."

- Consistent naming makes it easier for teams to navigate the board quickly.

3. Limit Work in Progress (WIP)

- Avoid having too many tasks in the "In Progress" list at once.

- Set a limit (e.g., only 3-5 cards can be in progress at a time).

- This prevents overload and keeps the team focused on finishing tasks before starting new ones.

4. Utilize Labels for Better Organization

- Use color-coded labels to identify task priority or category.

- Example:

    o   Red = Urgent

    o   Yellow = In Review

    o   Green = Completed

- Labels help visualize task status at a glance.

5. Use Automation to Keep Lists Updated

- Trello's Butler automation can move cards between lists automatically.

- Example:

- o   When a task's due date is reached, move it to "Urgent".

- o   When a checklist is completed, move it to "Completed".

- Automating repetitive actions saves time and reduces errors.

Common List Structures in Trello

Different teams use Trello lists in unique ways, depending on their workflow needs. Here are some popular list structures that can help improve productivity.

1. The Standard To-Do Workflow

The most common way to use Trello is to organize lists into a **task flow**:

📌 **To-Do** → 📌 **In Progress** → 📌 **Done**

- **To-Do**: Tasks that need to be completed.

- **In Progress**: Tasks actively being worked on.

- **Done**: Completed tasks, ready to be archived.

This setup is perfect for project management, team collaboration, and personal productivity.

2. The Agile Development Workflow

For software development teams, Trello can support Agile methodologies like Scrum or Kanban. A typical Agile workflow includes:

📌 **Backlog** → 📌 **Sprint Planning** → 📌 **In Development** → 📌 **Testing** → 📌 **Completed**

- Backlog: Upcoming tasks.

- Sprint Planning: Tasks selected for the next sprint.

- In Development: Tasks actively being worked on by developers.

- Testing: Quality assurance and debugging phase.

- Completed: Fully finished features.

This structure ensures a smooth development cycle and aligns with Agile best practices.

3. The Content Calendar Workflow

For marketing teams and content creators, Trello is often used as an editorial calendar.

📌 Ideas → 📌 Writing → 📌 Editing → 📌 Scheduled → 📌 Published

- Ideas: Initial brainstorming for blog posts, videos, or social media content.

- Writing: Content currently being created.

- Editing: Content under review before publication.

- Scheduled: Ready for publishing at a set date.

- Published: Content that is live and shared.

Using Trello for content management keeps teams aligned and ensures consistent publishing schedules.

Final Thoughts

Lists in Trello play a crucial role in structuring workflows, keeping tasks organized, and improving productivity. By effectively creating, managing, and customizing lists, users can streamline projects, enhance collaboration, and stay on top of their workload.

Key takeaways from this section:

✅ **Lists structure your work** and provide clear workflow stages.
✅ **Best practices** include naming conventions, limiting work in progress, and using automation.
✅ **Different workflows** cater to different needs, from project management to content planning.

Now that you understand how to use lists in Trello effectively, let's move on to the next section: Cards – Managing Individual Tasks!

2.2.2 Common List Structures (To-Do, In Progress, Done)

Trello's lists are one of its most essential features, providing a structured way to organize tasks and track their progress. While users can create custom workflows tailored to their needs, one of the most widely used list structures is the To-Do, In Progress, Done format.

This simple yet effective structure helps teams and individuals stay organized by clearly defining the stages of a task. In this section, we will explore:

- The importance of structured workflows

- The To-Do, In Progress, Done framework and how it works

- Best practices for using this system effectively

- How to customize this structure to fit different workflows

By the end of this section, you'll understand why this time-tested method is widely adopted and how you can use it to maximize your efficiency in Trello.

Why Structured Workflows Matter

Before diving into the specifics of the To-Do, In Progress, Done framework, let's discuss why structured workflows are critical for productivity.

Without a clear workflow, tasks can:
✓ Become disorganized and easily forgotten
✓ Lead to confusion among team members
✓ Cause missed deadlines and inefficiencies
✓ Create bottlenecks in project execution

Using a well-defined structure like To-Do, In Progress, Done, you can:
✓ Visualize the progress of your tasks
✓ Ensure accountability by clearly assigning work
✓ Minimize confusion about the status of tasks
✓ Streamline collaboration between teams

Now, let's break down how this framework works in Trello.

Breaking Down the To-Do, In Progress, Done Framework

The To-Do, In Progress, Done framework is based on the Kanban method, a workflow management technique designed to help teams visualize and optimize their work process.

📌 To-Do List

The To-Do list acts as a backlog of all tasks that need to be completed. It serves as the starting point for every project.

How to use it:

- Create a **card** for each task that needs to be completed.

- Assign **due dates** to indicate priority levels.

- Add **checklists** if a task requires multiple steps.

- Attach **documents, images, or links** related to the task.

- Use **labels** (e.g., "High Priority," "Low Priority") to categorize tasks.

Example To-Do List in Trello:

✅ Write an article on "Trello Best Practices" (Due: March 30)

✅ Research competitor project management tools (Due: April 2)

✅ Update client presentation slides (Due: April 5)

By keeping all pending tasks in the To-Do list, you ensure that nothing gets forgotten and that team members know what needs attention.

___

□□ In Progress List

The In Progress list contains tasks that are actively being worked on. This helps team members stay aligned on what is currently in motion.

How to use it:

- Move a task from the To-Do list to the In Progress list when work begins.

- Assign a team member to indicate responsibility.

- Add comments and updates as progress is made.

- Use due dates and checklists to track progress.

Example In Progress List in Trello:
☐ Writing blog post draft (Assigned: John | Due: March 30)
☐ Reviewing client proposal (Assigned: Sarah | Due: April 1)
☐ Editing marketing video (Assigned: Alex | Due: April 3)

This list provides real-time insight into the work being done, helping teams track progress and avoid bottlenecks.

✅ Done List

The Done list contains completed tasks. This provides a sense of accomplishment and serves as a record of completed work.

How to use it:

- Move a **task** from the **In Progress list** to the **Done list** once it is completed.

- Keep a **comment history** to track any final changes made.

- Use **archiving** if the list becomes too long and cluttered.

- If needed, apply **filters** to track work completed within a specific time frame.

Example Done List in Trello:
✅ Published "Trello Best Practices" article (Completed: March 30)
✅ Sent revised proposal to client (Completed: April 1)
✅ Uploaded marketing video to YouTube (Completed: April 3)

By maintaining a Done list, teams can track progress over time and review completed work for future reference.

Best Practices for Using To-Do, In Progress, Done

While the **To-Do, In Progress, Done** framework is simple, applying best practices can further enhance its effectiveness.

1⬚ Keep Lists Clear and Concise

- Avoid overloading the To-Do list with too many tasks.
- Keep task descriptions clear and actionable.

2⬚ Use Due Dates and Reminders

- Assign realistic deadlines to keep work on schedule.
- Use Trello's reminder notifications for upcoming deadlines.

3⬚ Assign Team Members and Responsibilities

- Ensure each task has an owner to avoid confusion.
- Use @mentions in comments to notify specific team members.

4⬚ Regularly Review and Update Lists

- Hold weekly team reviews to discuss progress.
- Remove irrelevant or outdated tasks from the board.

5⬚ Automate Repetitive Tasks with Butler

- Set up automation rules to move tasks when checklists are completed.
- Create custom buttons to trigger predefined actions.

By following these best practices, you can maximize the efficiency and clarity of your Trello workflow.

Customizing the To-Do, In Progress, Done Structure

While the To-Do, In Progress, Done model is effective, it may not fit every workflow exactly. Here are some ways to customize it for different needs.

📌 Adding More Workflow Stages

For more complex projects, you can add intermediate lists such as:

- Waiting for Approval (For tasks that need manager/client sign-off)

- On Hold (For tasks delayed due to dependencies)

- Testing/Review (For software development or quality assurance workflows)

📌 Using Labels for Task Categorization

- Use labels like "Urgent," "High Priority," or "Low Priority" to indicate importance.

- Categorize tasks by departments (e.g., Marketing, Sales, Development).

📌 Creating Separate Boards for Large Projects

If your project involves multiple teams, consider creating separate Trello boards for different teams while maintaining a master board for high-level tracking.

Final Thoughts

The To-Do, In Progress, Done workflow is one of the most effective ways to manage tasks in Trello. Its simplicity, flexibility, and clarity make it ideal for individuals and teams alike.

By using this structure, you can:
✓ Stay organized and track progress efficiently.
✓ Improve team collaboration by keeping tasks visible.
✓ Reduce confusion with a clear workflow.

Now that you understand how to structure your lists effectively, the next section will explore how to manage individual tasks using Trello cards. 🚀

2.3 Cards: Managing Individual Tasks

2.3.1 Adding and Editing Cards

Trello's core functionality revolves around cards, which represent individual tasks, ideas, or pieces of information. Cards are the building blocks of Trello boards, allowing users to organize, track, and manage work efficiently. Whether you're planning a project, creating a content calendar, or tracking a personal to-do list, understanding how to add and edit cards effectively is essential.

In this section, we will explore:

✓ How to add new cards to a Trello board.

✓ How to edit and customize cards.

✓ How to use advanced card features for better task management.

What is a Trello Card?

A Trello card represents a single task, idea, or work item within a list on a Trello board. Each card can contain detailed information, including descriptions, checklists, due dates, attachments, comments, and more.

Key Features of a Trello Card:

📌 **Title** – A brief name for the task.

📌 **Description** – Additional details about the task.

📌 **Labels** – Color-coded tags for easy categorization.

📌 **Checklists** – Subtasks to break down work into smaller steps.

📌 **Due Dates** – Deadlines to keep track of important tasks.

📌 **Attachments** – Files, images, and links related to the task.

📌 **Comments & Mentions** – Collaboration features for team discussions.

📌 **Activity Log** – A history of actions taken on the card.

Now, let's go step by step on **how to add and edit cards in Trello**.

Adding a New Card to a Trello Board

Step 1: Navigate to the List Where You Want to Add a Card

- Open your **Trello board**.

- Locate the list where you want to add a new card (e.g., **To-Do, In Progress, Done**).

Step 2: Click "Add a Card"

- At the bottom of any list, you will see an **"Add a card"** button.

- Click on it, and a text box will appear for you to enter the **card title**.

Step 3: Enter a Title and Click "Add Card"

- Type a **clear and concise** card title, such as:

  - "Write Trello tutorial chapter"

  - "Review client proposal"

  - "Plan team meeting agenda"

- Press **Enter** or click the **"Add Card"** button to create the card.

◆ *Pro Tip:* Use **actionable titles** to make tasks clearer. Instead of "Meeting," write "Schedule a team meeting for Monday."

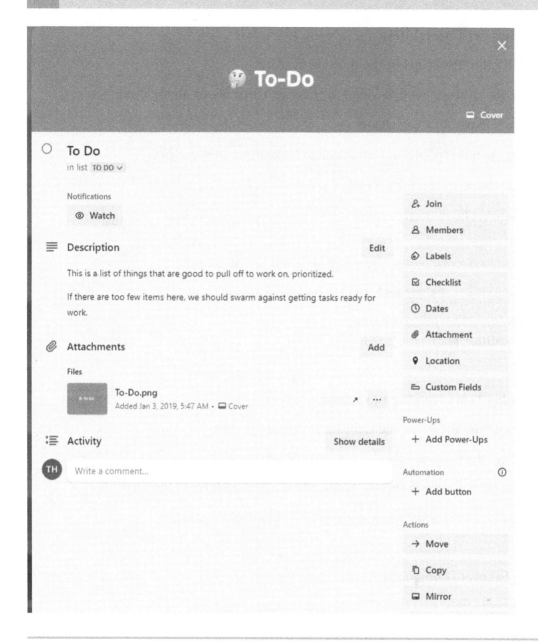

Editing and Customizing Trello Cards

Once a card is added, you can **customize and edit** it to provide more details. Click on a card to open it and access its features.

1️⃣ Adding a Card Description

- Click the **"Description"** field inside the card.

- Write additional details about the task, instructions, or any relevant notes.

- Click **"Save"** to apply changes.

◆ *Pro Tip:* Use bullet points or formatting to make descriptions clear.

📌 Example Description for a Trello Card:

Task: Create Trello tutorial chapter
Details:

- Write a detailed guide on adding and editing Trello cards.

- Include screenshots and step-by-step instructions.

- Proofread before submission.
  Deadline: March 30, 2025

2️⃣ Assigning Team Members to a Card

- Click **"Members"** on the right-hand side of the card.

- Select the team member(s) responsible for the task.

- Assigned users will receive notifications about updates to the card.

☐ *Use this feature to assign ownership and accountability for tasks!*

3️⃣ Using Labels to Categorize Cards

- Click **"Labels"** and select a color-coded label.

- Labels help in **categorizing tasks**, such as:

  - ⬤ Urgent

  - ☐ In Progress

  - ☐ Needs Review

- o ● High Priority

📌 *Pro Tip:* You can customize labels with text to make them more meaningful!

4️⃣ Adding a Checklist to Break Down Tasks

- Click **"Checklist"** and enter a name (e.g., "Subtasks").

- Add checklist items one by one.

- Mark items as complete as you progress.

✅ Example Checklist for a Blog Writing Task:

☑ Research the topic
☑ Outline key points
☑ Write the first draft
☑ Edit and proofread
☑ Publish the post

5️⃣ Setting Due Dates and Reminders

- Click **"Due Date"** to set a deadline.

- Choose a date and time.

- Enable **reminders** to get notifications before the deadline.

🕐 *This helps teams stay on schedule and prioritize tasks effectively!*

6️⃣ Attaching Files, Links, and Images

- Click **"Attachments"** to upload files from:

  - o 💼 Your computer

  - o ☁ Google Drive, Dropbox, or OneDrive

  - o 🔗 A web link

📌 *Example:* Attach a **PDF report** to a "Review Client Proposal" card.

7️⃣ Adding Comments and Mentions for Collaboration

- Click **"Comment"** to add updates or ask questions.
- Use **@mentions** to notify specific team members.

💬 **Example:**

- **@John** Can you review this by tomorrow?
- **@Team** Let's finalize this by Friday.

8️⃣ Moving, Copying, and Archiving Cards

Trello allows you to **move, copy, or archive** cards as needed.

📌 **Moving a Card:**

- Drag the card to a different list (e.g., from "To-Do" to "In Progress").

📌 **Copying a Card:**

- Click the **"Copy"** option to duplicate a card with similar content.

📌 **Archiving a Card:**

- Click **"Archive"** to remove completed tasks from the board.

🚀 *This helps keep your board clean and organized!*

Best Practices for Managing Trello Cards Effectively

✓ Keep card titles clear and concise.
✓ Use labels and due dates for better organization.
✓ Break down complex tasks with checklists.
✓ Assign team members to ensure accountability.

✓ Use comments and mentions for team communication.

✓ Archive completed cards to declutter your board.

By mastering the adding and editing of Trello cards, you can enhance productivity, improve task management, and streamline collaboration within your team.

Conclusion

In this section, we explored how to add and edit Trello cards efficiently. We covered:

✓ Creating new cards and structuring tasks effectively.

✓ Editing and customizing cards with descriptions, labels, and checklists.

✓ Assigning members, setting due dates, and adding attachments.

✓ Using Trello's collaboration features for better teamwork.

Now that you've mastered cards, let's move on to the next section, where we will learn how to move, archive, and manage Trello cards more efficiently!

2.3.2 Moving Cards Between Lists

In Trello, cards represent individual tasks, ideas, or pieces of information that move through different stages of a workflow. One of the most powerful aspects of Trello is its ability to allow seamless movement of cards between lists, enabling users to visualize progress, manage workload efficiently, and keep projects organized.

This section will provide a detailed guide on how to move cards between lists, the different methods available, best practices for efficient task management, and real-world examples of workflow optimization.

Why Moving Cards Between Lists is Important

Moving cards in Trello is more than just rearranging tasks—it helps teams and individuals track the progress of a project visually and ensures that work is being completed in an organized manner. Here's why it's important:

✓ **Tracks task progress:** Moving a card from "To-Do" to "In Progress" to "Done" gives clear visibility into a project's status.

✅ **Helps prioritize work:** Tasks can be rearranged within lists based on urgency and importance.

✅ **Improves workflow efficiency:** Cards can be assigned to different team members or moved to different categories for better task delegation.

✅ **Encourages accountability:** Team members know exactly what stage a task is in and who is responsible for it.

✅ **Keeps workspaces organized:** Moving completed tasks to an archive list keeps the board clean and clutter-free.

How to Move Cards Between Lists in Trello

There are several ways to move cards between lists in Trello, each offering different levels of control and customization.

Method 1: Drag-and-Drop (Most Common Method)

The easiest and most intuitive way to move a card in Trello is by dragging and dropping it from one list to another.

Steps to Move a Card Using Drag-and-Drop:

1. Open your Trello board.

2. Locate the card you want to move.

3. Click and hold the card.

4. Drag the card to the desired list and drop it at the preferred position.

5. Release the mouse, and the card will be placed in the new list.

This method is quick, visual, and effective for users who need to manage their workflow dynamically.

✅ **Best for:** Daily task updates, simple task tracking, and small teams managing straightforward workflows.

Method 2: Using the "Move" Option from the Card Menu

If you need more control over where a card is moved, or if you're managing a large board with many lists, using the **"Move"** feature in the card menu is a great option.

Steps to Move a Card Using the "Move" Option:

1. Open the Trello board where the card is located.

2. Click on the card you want to move.

3. In the card window, click on **"Move"** from the right-hand menu.

4. Select the destination **board (if moving to another board)** and the **list** where you want to place the card.

5. Choose the exact **position** where you want the card to appear in the list.

6. Click **"Move"**, and the card will be transferred instantly.

✅ **Best for:** Moving cards between different boards, ensuring precise placement within a list, and handling complex workflows.

Method 3: Using Keyboard Shortcuts for Faster Movement

For power users who want to move cards quickly, Trello offers keyboard shortcuts to streamline the process.

Keyboard Shortcuts for Moving Cards:

- Press **"C"** to close a card (archive it).

- Press **"M"** to open the "Move" menu quickly.

- Use the **arrow keys** to select the list and position where you want the card to move.

- Press **"Enter"** to confirm the move.

✅ **Best for:** Users who prefer keyboard commands over mouse actions and those managing a high volume of tasks.

Method 4: Automating Card Movements with Butler (Trello's Automation Tool)

For **repetitive tasks**, Trello's **Butler automation tool** can automatically move cards based on certain triggers or conditions.

Examples of Automating Card Movement with Butler:

- Move a card to the "In Progress" list when a user is added to the card.

- Automatically move a card to the "Done" list when a due date is marked as complete.

- Send overdue tasks to a special list for review.

Steps to Automate Card Movements Using Butler:

1. Open Trello and go to the board where you want to set up automation.

2. Click on **"Automation"** (found in the top menu).

3. Select **"Rules"** and click **"Create Rule"**.

4. Set a trigger (e.g., "When a due date is marked complete").

5. Define an action (e.g., "Move the card to the Done list").

6. Save the rule, and Trello will now automatically move cards based on this condition.

✅ **Best for:** Teams managing complex workflows, repetitive task movements, and process automation.

Best Practices for Moving Cards in Trello

To make the most of Trello's flexibility, follow these **best practices** when moving cards between lists:

1. Establish a Clear Workflow Structure

- Define standardized list names (e.g., "To-Do," "In Progress," "Done") to maintain clarity.

- Set up special lists for high-priority tasks or urgent items.

2. Use Labels to Categorize Tasks

- Assign **color-coded labels** to indicate task priority (e.g., red for urgent, green for low priority).

- Apply labels to group similar tasks together.

3. Keep Lists Manageable

- Avoid overcrowding lists with too many cards. Move completed or inactive tasks to an **archive list**.

- If a list becomes too long, break it into **smaller, focused lists** for better organization.

4. Use Due Dates and Notifications

- Ensure that **moving cards** triggers reminders or updates for team members.

- Set due dates so tasks don't get lost in the workflow.

5. Review and Adjust Regularly

- Conduct **weekly reviews** to reorganize lists and ensure tasks are in the right place.

- Adjust workflows based on team needs and project complexity.

Real-World Examples of Moving Cards Effectively

Example 1: Software Development Team

A software development team might have the following Trello workflow:

📌 **Backlog → To-Do → In Development → Testing → Done**

As tasks progress, developers move cards **from left to right**, ensuring the entire team knows which features are being worked on.

Example 2: Content Marketing Team

A marketing team managing blog content could structure Trello like this:

📝 **Ideas → Writing → Editing → Ready to Publish → Published**

Writers move articles across the board as they complete different stages of content creation.

Final Thoughts

Moving cards between lists in Trello is a simple yet powerful feature that helps individuals and teams stay organized, track progress, and optimize productivity.

By using drag-and-drop, the Move option, keyboard shortcuts, and automation, you can effectively manage workflows and ensure tasks are completed on time.

Now that you understand how to move cards efficiently, the next section will cover archiving and deleting cards—another essential aspect of maintaining an organized Trello board.

🚀 Ready to master more Trello features? Let's continue!

2.3.3 Archiving and Deleting Cards

Trello's archiving and deleting features allow users to keep their boards clean, organized, and free of clutter. Properly managing old or unnecessary cards helps streamline workflows and ensures that your team focuses on current and relevant tasks. However, many new Trello users are unsure about the differences between archiving and deleting and how to use these functions effectively.

In this section, we will explore the differences between archiving and deleting cards, how to archive cards, restore them if needed, and permanently delete them from your board. Additionally, we'll cover best practices to maintain a well-organized Trello board.

The Difference Between Archiving and Deleting Cards

Before we dive into the mechanics of archiving and deleting, it's crucial to understand the key difference between these two actions:

Feature	Archiving	Deleting
Definition	Moves a card out of sight but keeps it accessible for future reference.	Permanently removes the card from Trello with no way to recover it.
Recoverability	Yes, archived cards can be restored at any time.	No, deleted cards **cannot** be restored.

Best Use Case	When you don't need a card now but may need it later.	When you are 100% sure the card is no longer needed.

For most users, archiving is a safer option than deleting, as it allows you to retrieve the card later if necessary. Deletion should be reserved for cards that are completely unnecessary and will never be needed again.

How to Archive Cards in Trello

Archiving a Single Card

Archiving a card is straightforward. Follow these steps:

1. Open the Trello board that contains the card you want to archive.

2. Locate the card and click on it to open its details.

3. Click on the **"Archive"** button located at the bottom-right of the card menu.

4. The card will disappear from the board but will be stored in the archive.

If you need to archive multiple cards at once, you must **repeat the process for each card**, as Trello does not currently support bulk archiving.

Accessing Archived Cards

If you ever need to revisit an archived card:

1. Click on the **"Show Menu"** button in the top-right corner of your Trello board.

2. Select **"More"** and then click on **"Archived Items"**.

3. Browse through the archived cards or use the search bar to find a specific card.

Restoring an Archived Card

To bring an archived card back to your board:

1. Navigate to the **Archived Items** menu as described above.

2. Locate the card you want to restore.

3. Click **"Send to board"**, and the card will return to its original position.

This feature is particularly useful for tasks that may be temporarily inactive but could be needed again later.

How to Delete Cards in Trello

If you are absolutely certain that a card is no longer needed, you can delete it permanently. However, Trello does not provide a direct "Delete" button on active cards. Instead, you must first archive the card before you can delete it.

Steps to Permanently Delete a Card

1. **Archive the card**: Open the card, then click on **"Archive"** at the bottom.

2. **Click on "Delete"**: Once the card is archived, a **"Delete"** option will appear next to the **"Send to board"** button.

3. **Confirm deletion**: Click **"Delete"**, and Trello will ask you to confirm. Once confirmed, the card will be permanently erased.

Deleting Cards in Bulk

Trello does not offer a bulk delete option by default, but you can speed up the process using third-party Power-Ups like:

- Butler for Trello (Automate repetitive actions, including archiving and deleting)

- Card Delete Power-Up (Enables direct deletion without archiving first)

Using these Power-Ups can save time when handling large numbers of completed or irrelevant tasks.

Best Practices for Archiving and Deleting Cards

To maintain an organized and efficient Trello board, follow these best practices when handling old tasks:

1. Archive Instead of Delete (When in Doubt)

- If you're unsure whether a card will be needed in the future, archive it instead of deleting it.

- This ensures you can retrieve valuable information if circumstances change.

2. Use Labels or Tags Before Archiving

- Apply a label (e.g., "Completed", "Obsolete") to a card before archiving it.

- This helps track archived items for future reference.

3. Create an "Archived Tasks" List (Alternative to Archiving)

- Instead of archiving, you can create a "Completed Tasks" or "Archived" list on your board.

- This keeps tasks visible but separate from active workflows.

4. Regularly Clean Up Archived Items

- Periodically review your archived items and permanently delete anything that is no longer needed.

- This prevents unnecessary clutter and improves board performance.

5. Automate Archiving for Recurring Tasks

- Use Butler Automation to automatically archive completed tasks after a set period.

- Example: Move all cards in the "Done" list to the archive after 7 days.

These strategies will help you manage Trello efficiently without losing important information.

Summary: Keeping Your Trello Board Organized

Mastering archiving and deleting cards is crucial for keeping your Trello board clean, efficient, and easy to navigate. Here's a quick recap:

✓ Archive cards when they are no longer needed but might be useful later.
✓ Restore archived cards from the Archived Items menu when necessary.
✓ Delete cards only when you are certain they won't be needed again.
✓ Use automation tools like Butler to streamline the process.
✓ Regularly clean up your archive to prevent unnecessary clutter.

By implementing these best practices, you will ensure that your Trello board remains structured, effective, and optimized for productivity.

What's Next?

Now that you know how to **archive and delete cards effectively**, the next section will explore **advanced card features**, such as adding attachments, using due dates, and setting up reminders to keep your tasks on track.

Are you ready to take your **Trello skills to the next level**? Let's move on! 🚀

CHAPTER III
Enhancing Your Trello Experience

3.1 Labels, Checklists, and Due Dates

3.1.1 Using Labels to Categorize Tasks

Trello's **labels** are a powerful tool for categorizing and organizing tasks. They provide **visual indicators** that help users quickly identify and prioritize tasks. By using labels effectively, you can streamline workflows, improve task tracking, and enhance collaboration within teams.

In this section, we will explore:

- What Trello labels are and why they are useful

- How to create, customize, and apply labels

- Practical ways to use labels for task management

- Best practices for using labels efficiently

What Are Trello Labels?

Trello labels are color-coded tags that can be attached to cards. They serve as quick visual markers that help users categorize tasks based on different criteria, such as priority, task type, project phase, or assigned department.

Each label has a color and can have an optional text description to specify its meaning. Trello provides 10 default colors, but users can assign their own meanings to these colors.

For example:

Label Color Example Usage

● **Red**   High Priority

☐ **Yellow**   Medium Priority

☐ **Green**   Completed

◕ **Blue**   In Progress

☐ **Purple**   Needs Review

☐ **Orange**   Waiting for Approval

Since Trello allows multiple labels per card, you can apply **more than one category** to a single task.

Why Use Labels in Trello?

1. Quick Visual Organization

- Labels make it easy to **scan a board and understand task statuses at a glance**.
- They reduce the need to open each card individually to check details.

2. Improved Prioritization

- You can use labels to **highlight urgent tasks** and differentiate between high, medium, and low-priority items.
- This helps teams focus on **critical** tasks first.

3. Streamlined Filtering and Searching

- Trello allows you to **filter cards** by label, making it easier to find specific tasks.
- If you manage large boards with many tasks, labels help to **narrow down** what you're looking for.

4. Enhanced Collaboration

- Team members can use labels to **indicate task ownership, project phases, or types of work**.

- Everyone on the team can quickly understand task categories without extensive explanations.

How to Create and Customize Labels in Trello

Trello makes it easy to create, edit, and apply labels to cards. Follow these steps to start using labels effectively:

Step 1: Adding a Label to a Card

1. Open a **Trello board** and navigate to a **card**.

2. Click on the **card** to open its details.

3. Select **"Labels"** from the right-hand menu.

4. Choose an **existing label** or click **"Create a new label"**.

5. Pick a **color** and enter a **name/description** for the label.

6. Click **"Save"** and the label will now be added to the card.

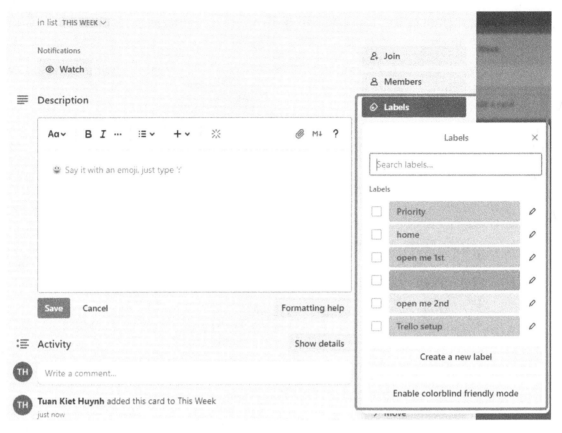

Step 2: Editing or Deleting a Label

1. Open a card and click **"Labels"**.

2. Hover over the label you want to edit and click the **pencil icon**.

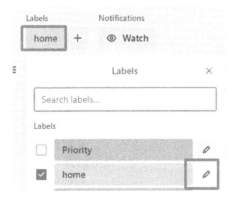

3. Change the **color or text**, then click **"Save"**.

4. To delete a label, simply **remove it from all cards** where it has been applied.

Step 3: Filtering Cards by Label

1. On the **Trello board**, click **"Filter"** at the top right.

2. Select the **label(s)** you want to filter by.

3. Trello will now **only display cards** that contain the selected labels.

This feature is useful when working with **large projects**, as it allows you to focus on specific types of tasks.

Practical Ways to Use Labels in Trello

1. Prioritizing Tasks

- Use labels to indicate task urgency:

- ○ ● **Red** = Urgent

- ○ ☐ **Yellow** = Medium Priority

- ○ ☐ **Green** = Low Priority

- This method ensures that **critical tasks** are tackled first while less urgent ones are scheduled accordingly.

2. Categorizing Task Types

- Assign labels based on different **types of work**:

    - ○ ☐ **Purple** = Administrative tasks

    - ○ ● **Blue** = Creative work

    - ○ ☐ **Orange** = Client-related tasks

- This helps teams quickly identify the nature of a task without reading through details.

3. Organizing Project Phases

- Large projects often go through multiple stages:

    - ○ ☐ **Green** = Planning

    - ○ ☐ **Yellow** = In Progress

    - ○ ● **Red** = Requires Review

    - ○ ☐ **Purple** = Completed

- With this setup, teams can easily track progress and identify bottlenecks.

4. Assigning Labels by Department or Team

- For cross-functional teams, labels can indicate which department is responsible for a task:

    - ○ ● **Blue** = Marketing

    - ○ ☐ **Green** = Development

    - ○ ☐ **Orange** = Sales

- ○ ☐ **Yellow** = Customer Support
- This makes it **clear who is responsible** for each card without needing additional text descriptions.

5. Using Labels for Client Management

- If you manage multiple clients, labels can differentiate tasks by client:
  - ○ ☐ **Purple** = Client A
  - ○ ⬤ **Blue** = Client B
  - ○ ☐ **Orange** = Client C
- This ensures that tasks stay organized and separated by client projects.

Best Practices for Using Labels in Trello

✓ Keep label categories consistent – Avoid unnecessary label variations to prevent confusion.
✓ Use color-coding logically – Make sure the meaning of each color is clear to all team members.
✓ Limit the number of labels per card – Too many labels can make cards harder to read.
✓ Regularly review and update labels – Keep your labeling system relevant as your workflow evolves.
✓ Communicate label meanings to your team – Ensure everyone understands the purpose of each label.

By following these best practices, you can maximize the efficiency of labels in Trello.

Summary: Mastering Task Categorization with Labels

Using labels in Trello helps you:

- Organize tasks visually for quick identification
- Prioritize work efficiently by marking urgent and non-urgent tasks
- Filter tasks easily for better focus and workflow management

- Enhance team collaboration by providing clear task categorization

By leveraging Trello's labeling system, you can keep your projects structured, organized, and easy to manage.

Next, we will explore another essential feature of Trello: Checklists for Task Management.

3.1.2 Creating Checklists for Task Management

Task management is a crucial aspect of any workflow, whether you're working on a personal project, managing a team, or overseeing complex business operations. One of the most effective ways to break down tasks into manageable steps is by using **checklists**. Trello provides a built-in checklist feature that helps users organize tasks within individual cards, ensuring that no steps are overlooked.

In this section, we will cover:
✓ The importance of checklists in task management
✓ How to create and use checklists in Trello
✓ Best practices for structuring effective checklists
✓ Advanced checklist features such as automation and integrations

By the end of this section, you'll understand how to maximize the use of **Trello checklists** to boost productivity and keep your workflow organized.

Why Use Checklists in Trello?

Checklists are powerful tools that help individuals and teams break down complex tasks into smaller, actionable steps. Here are some key benefits of using checklists in Trello:

- **Increased productivity**: Having a clear list of tasks ensures that everything gets done efficiently.

- **Better organization**: Large tasks can be overwhelming, but checklists make them more structured.

- **Improved team collaboration**: Team members can check off completed items, keeping everyone informed.

- **Reduced errors and missed tasks**: Ensuring that every required step is completed prevents mistakes.

- **Clear progress tracking**: You can see at a glance how much work has been completed.

Checklists are useful in a variety of scenarios, including project planning, content creation, event organization, software development, customer support, and more.

How to Create a Checklist in Trello

Trello makes it incredibly simple to create checklists within a card. Follow these steps to add a checklist to your tasks:

Step 1: Open a Trello Card

1. Navigate to your **Trello board**.

2. Click on a **card** where you want to add a checklist.

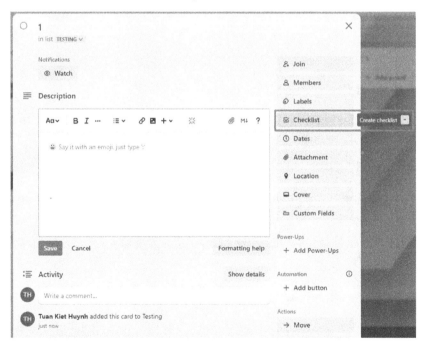

Step 2: Add a Checklist

1. Inside the card, click on the **"Checklist"** button in the right-hand menu.

2. Enter a name for your checklist (e.g., "Project Steps" or "To-Do List") or leave the default name as "Checklist".

3. Click **"Add"**, and your checklist will appear inside the card.

Step 3: Add Items to the Checklist

1. Type in an item and press **Enter** to add it to the checklist.

2. Continue adding items as needed.

3. To reorder checklist items, simply **drag and drop** them.

Step 4: Check Off Completed Items

- When a task is completed, click the **checkbox** next to the item to mark it as done.

- Trello automatically tracks **progress percentage**, showing how many items are completed.

This simple process helps you create **well-structured checklists** that make managing tasks effortless.

Best Practices for Structuring Effective Checklists

Creating a checklist is easy, but making an **effective** checklist requires planning. Here are some tips to ensure your checklists enhance productivity:

1. Keep Items Actionable and Specific

- ✓ Instead of "Marketing Campaign," write "Create ad copy for Facebook campaign."

- ✓ Instead of "Prepare Meeting," write "Send meeting invite and agenda by Monday."

- Avoid vague checklist items that don't clearly define an action.

2. Use Checklists for Task Breakdown

- Large tasks should be split into smaller, manageable steps.
- Example: Instead of "Launch Product Website," create:
    - ✅ Purchase domain
    - ✅ Design homepage
    - ✅ Test mobile responsiveness
    - ✅ Publish site

3. Prioritize Items in the Checklist

- Place **urgent** or **important** tasks at the top.
- Use labels or numbering if necessary:
    - ⬤ High Priority
    - ☐ Medium Priority
    - ☐ Low Priority

4. Assign Responsibility for Each Item

- Trello does not allow direct assignments within checklists, but you can:
    - Mention team members in comments (e.g., "@John, please review this").
    - Convert checklist items into **separate cards** and assign members to those.

5. Use Multiple Checklists When Needed

- For complex projects, you can create **multiple checklists** within a card.

- Example: A card titled "Website Launch" might have:

    o 💅 Checklist 1: Design Tasks

    o ✅ Checklist 2: Content Creation

    o 🔍 Checklist 3: SEO and Testing

By following these best practices, you ensure your checklists are clear, actionable, and effective.

Advanced Checklist Features in Trello

1. Converting Checklist Items into Cards

- If a checklist item becomes too complex, click the "Convert to Card" option to move it to the main board.

- This helps with task delegation and better visibility.

2. Automating Checklists with Butler

Trello's Butler automation tool allows you to:

- Automatically create checklists when a card is added to a list.

- Move checklist items to a new card once completed.

- Assign due dates based on checklist completion.

Example automation rule:

"When a card is moved to 'In Progress,' add a checklist named 'Development Tasks.'"

3. Integrating Checklists with Power-Ups

Enhance checklists using Trello Power-Ups:

- Custom Fields: Add extra details to checklist items.

- Calendar View: See checklist due dates in a calendar format.

- Task Dependencies: Use integrations like Planyway or Hello Epics to track dependencies.

Real-World Examples of Using Trello Checklists

Checklists can be applied in numerous industries and workflows:

Example 1: Project Management

A project manager at a **marketing agency** might create a card for a campaign with a checklist:
✓ Define target audience
✓ Create marketing materials
✓ Launch social media ads
✓ Monitor engagement

Example 2: Event Planning

A **wedding planner** might use a checklist to ensure all preparations are complete:
✓ Book venue
✓ Send invitations
✓ Arrange catering
✓ Confirm guest list

Example 3: Software Development

A **developer team** could track development tasks using:
✓ Write code
✓ Run unit tests
✓ Deploy to staging
✓ Perform QA testing

By using checklists, professionals in **any industry** can improve efficiency and ensure **every step is completed**.

Conclusion: Making the Most of Checklists in Trello

Checklists are one of the most powerful yet simple features in Trello. They help users:
✓☐ Break down large tasks into manageable steps
✓☐ Track progress at a glance

✓☐ Collaborate efficiently with teams

✓☐ Automate repetitive actions for greater efficiency

By implementing structured and well-organized checklists, you can streamline your workflow and boost productivity in both personal and professional projects.

In the next section, we'll explore how to set and manage due dates in Trello, ensuring that tasks are completed on time and projects stay on track. 🚀

3.1.3 Setting and Managing Due Dates

Managing deadlines effectively is crucial for keeping tasks on track, ensuring accountability, and improving overall workflow efficiency. Trello provides a simple yet powerful due date feature that helps individuals and teams stay organized by clearly defining task deadlines. In this section, we will explore how to set, modify, and manage due dates in Trello, as well as best practices for deadline management and how to use automation tools to streamline the process.

Understanding Due Dates in Trello

Due dates in Trello are associated with **cards**, which represent tasks or projects. A **due date** provides a **clear deadline** for a task and can be used to track progress, set reminders, and ensure timely completion. Trello allows users to:

✅ Set due dates for tasks and projects.

✅ Receive notifications and reminders before deadlines.

✅ Filter and sort cards based on due dates.

✅ Automate actions based on upcoming or overdue tasks.

Due dates are essential for project planning, prioritization, and ensuring **smooth workflow execution**.

How to Set Due Dates in Trello

Setting due dates in Trello is straightforward. Follow these steps to add a due date to a Trello card:

Step 1: Open the Trello Card

- Navigate to the board where your task is located.

- Click on the **card** to open the detailed view.

Step 2: Click on the "Due Date" Option

- In the card menu on the right-hand side, you will see a **"Due Date"** button. Click on it.

Step 3: Select the Deadline

- A calendar will appear, allowing you to **choose a specific date and time** for the task's completion.

- The default time is **12:00 PM**, but you can modify it as needed.

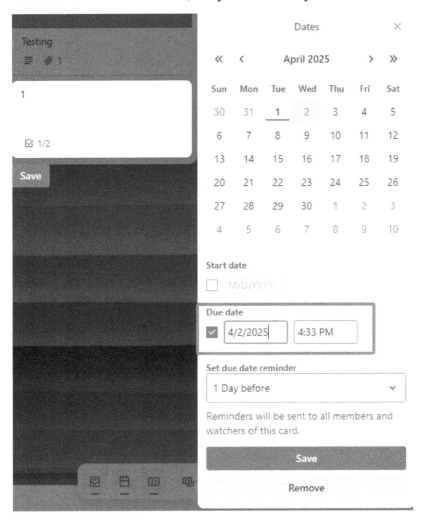

Step 4: Confirm the Due Date

- Click **Save** to apply the due date to the card.

- The selected due date will now be visible on the card.

How to Manage and Modify Due Dates

Once a due date is set, you may need to adjust it based on project needs. Here's how to manage and modify due dates in Trello:

Editing a Due Date

- Open the card containing the due date.
- Click on the existing **due date field**.
- Select a new date and time from the calendar.
- Click **Save** to update the due date.

Marking a Task as Completed

- Once a task is finished, open the card and **check the box** next to the due date.
- The due date will **turn green**, indicating the task is complete.
- This is useful for keeping track of progress and maintaining clarity within the team.

Removing a Due Date

- If a due date is no longer needed, click on the due date and select **Remove**.
- This removes the deadline from the card without deleting the task.

Using Due Dates for Task Prioritization

Trello offers several ways to **prioritize tasks** based on due dates, ensuring that high-priority tasks get the attention they need.

Sorting Cards by Due Date

- On a Trello board, click the **"Show Menu"** option.
- Select **"Sort by Due Date"** to arrange tasks from nearest to farthest deadlines.
- This helps you **quickly identify urgent tasks** and plan accordingly.

Color Coding for Urgency

- Trello automatically color-codes due dates:
  - ● **Red** – Overdue tasks.
  - ☐ **Orange** – Tasks due within 24 hours.
  - ☐ **Yellow** – Tasks due soon.
  - ☐ **Green** – Completed tasks.

- These visual indicators make it easy to see what needs immediate attention.

Filtering Tasks by Due Date

- Click on the **Search/Filter** icon.

- Use **filters** to display only tasks that are **due today, this week, or overdue**.

By combining sorting, filtering, and color-coding, users can effectively prioritize work and meet deadlines efficiently.

Setting Up Due Date Reminders and Notifications

Trello provides automatic notifications and reminders to keep users informed about upcoming deadlines.

Enabling Due Date Reminders

- Trello sends a default reminder 24 hours before a due date.

- Users can customize reminder times based on project needs.

Types of Due Date Notifications

🔔 Email Notifications – Receive reminders via email.
➡☐ Push Notifications – Get alerts on mobile and desktop apps.
☐ In-App Notifications – See reminders in Trello's notification center.

How to Customize Reminder Times

- Open the card and click the **due date**.

- Choose **"Set Reminder"** and select a custom notification time (e.g., **1 hour before, 1 day before, or custom**).

- Click **Save** to apply the reminder.

These notifications help users stay on top of deadlines and **avoid last-minute rushes**.

Automating Due Date Management with Butler

Trello's automation tool, Butler, can help automate due date-related tasks, reducing manual work.

Examples of Due Date Automations

⚡ Automatically move overdue tasks – If a task is overdue, Butler can move it to an "Urgent" list.

⚡ Send reminders via Slack or email – Butler can notify users when deadlines are approaching.

⚡ Auto-complete tasks – If a checklist is fully completed, Butler can automatically mark the card as done.

Setting Up an Automation in Butler

1️⃣ Open **Butler** from the Trello board menu.
2️⃣ Select **"Rules"** and click **"Create New Rule"**.

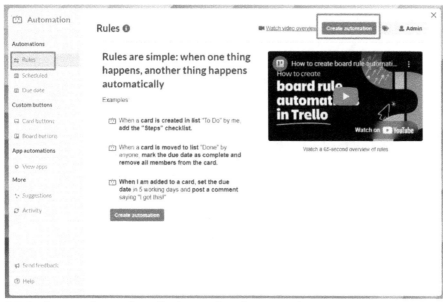

3️⃣ Define a **trigger** (e.g., "When a due date is 1 day away").

4️ Choose an **action** (e.g., "Move the card to the 'Urgent' list").

5️ Click **Save** to activate the rule.

With **automation**, teams can **minimize manual tracking** and focus on high-value tasks.

Best Practices for Managing Due Dates in Trello

To maximize the effectiveness of due dates, follow these best practices:

✓ Set realistic deadlines – Ensure due dates are achievable to avoid missed deadlines.

✓ Break down large tasks – Use checklists to divide complex projects into smaller, manageable parts.

✓ Use recurring tasks – Automate repetitive tasks with recurring due dates.

✓ Communicate with the team – Use comments and mentions to discuss due dates and potential changes.

✓ Regularly review due dates – Check Trello boards daily to stay on top of deadlines.

By implementing these strategies, you can improve productivity, reduce stress, and ensure smooth project execution.

Conclusion: Why Due Dates Matter

Due dates in Trello are a powerful tool for ensuring tasks are completed on time and projects run smoothly. Whether you're an individual tracking personal projects or a team managing complex workflows, using due dates effectively can:

✓ Increase accountability.

✓ Improve task prioritization.

✓ Reduce missed deadlines.

✓ Streamline workflow efficiency.

By leveraging due date reminders, filters, automation, and best practices, users can enhance their Trello experience and boost productivity.

Now that you understand how to set and manage due dates, let's move on to the next section: Attaching Files and Links to Cards, where we will explore how to enrich your Trello boards with relevant documents and resources.

3.2 Attaching Files and Links to Cards

3.2.1 Uploading Documents and Images

Trello is a powerful visual collaboration tool, and one of its most valuable features is the ability to attach files, documents, and images directly to Trello cards. This functionality makes it easy to store and access relevant materials, ensuring that team members have all the necessary resources in one place. Whether you're managing a project, tracking tasks, or organizing personal workflows, attaching files and images enhances your Trello experience by improving organization, streamlining communication, and reducing dependency on external storage solutions.

In this section, we will explore how to upload documents and images to Trello cards, discuss file size limitations, examine best practices for managing attachments, and review how to integrate cloud storage solutions for more efficient file handling.

Why Attach Files and Images to Trello Cards?

There are several key benefits to attaching files and images directly to Trello cards:

✅ **Centralized Storage** – Keep all necessary documents in one place, making it easier for team members to find what they need.

✅ **Improved Collaboration** – Share files with colleagues instantly, eliminating the need for long email threads.

✅ **Visual Representation** – Use images to illustrate ideas, track progress, or enhance project presentations.

✅ **Reduced Dependency on External Tools** – Instead of switching between multiple platforms, users can **access important documents** directly within Trello.

✅ **Version Control** – Keep track of the latest documents related to a specific task without searching through emails or shared drives.

By integrating file attachments, Trello helps teams and individuals **stay organized and efficient**, ensuring that essential information is always available at a glance.

How to Upload Files and Images to Trello Cards

Attaching files and images to Trello cards is simple and can be done in multiple ways. Let's go through the step-by-step process:

Step 1: Open the Trello Card

- Navigate to the Trello board where you want to attach a file or image.

- Click on the card to open its **detailed view**.

Step 2: Click the "Attach File" Button

- In the card's menu, locate the **"Attachments"** option.

- Click **"Attach File..."**, which allows you to select files from your device or cloud storage.

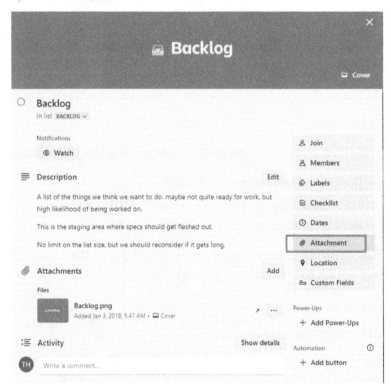

Step 3: Choose the File Source

You have multiple options for uploading files to Trello:

◆ Upload from Your Computer – Select a file from your local storage.

◆ Drag and Drop – Simply drag a file from your desktop and drop it onto the card.

◆ Attach from Cloud Storage – Connect to Google Drive, Dropbox, OneDrive, or Box to upload files directly.

◆ Paste a URL – If your document or image is hosted online, you can paste the link to attach it.

Step 4: Confirm Upload and View the File

- Once uploaded, the file appears under the "Attachments" section of the Trello card.

- Click the attachment to preview, download, or open it in a new tab.

- Trello will automatically generate a thumbnail preview for images and some document types (e.g., PDFs).

This process ensures that all relevant files are attached to the right tasks and can be accessed by team members instantly.

File Size Limitations and Restrictions

When uploading files to Trello, it's important to keep in mind the following size limitations:

✦ **Free Trello Plan:** Maximum file size per attachment is **10MB**.
✦ **Trello Standard and Premium:** Allows file attachments up to **250MB** per file.
✦ **Trello Enterprise:** Also supports file attachments up to **250MB** per file.

If you need to attach larger files, consider using Google Drive, Dropbox, or OneDrive, as these services allow Trello users to link to files without storage limitations.

Managing and Organizing Attachments

To avoid clutter and keep your Trello cards organized and efficient, follow these best practices:

📁 Use Clear File Names – Rename attachments with descriptive titles to make them easier to identify.
📁 Delete Outdated Files – Remove old attachments that are no longer relevant to the task.

📁 Use Labels or Comments for Context – Add comments or color labels to indicate file purpose or urgency.

📁 Integrate with Cloud Storage – For frequently updated documents, attach them from Google Drive or Dropbox instead of re-uploading new versions.

By implementing these strategies, teams can ensure quick access to essential documents without unnecessary clutter.

Attaching Images for Better Visualization

Images are extremely useful for project tracking, creative brainstorming, and team collaboration. Trello allows users to:

🖥️ Upload Screenshots – Perfect for software development teams tracking bugs.
🖥️ Attach Diagrams and Charts – Great for project planning, workflows, and reports.
🖥️ Use Image Covers – Set an image as the card cover to make it visually stand out.
🖥️ Preview Images Directly in Trello – No need to download; images can be viewed instantly within the Trello interface.

Using images within Trello enhances communication, creativity, and overall project clarity.

Integrating with Cloud Storage Services

For users who work with large files or require real-time collaboration on documents, integrating cloud storage with Trello is a game-changer.

Popular Cloud Storage Integrations:

- **Google Drive** – Attach Google Docs, Sheets, and Slides for live collaboration.

- **Dropbox** – Link files and sync updates seamlessly.

- **OneDrive** – Integrate with Microsoft 365 documents.

- **Box** – Securely store and share business files.

How to Attach Files from Cloud Storage:

1. Open a Trello card and click **"Attach File"**.

2. Select the cloud storage service you want to connect.

3. Sign in and choose the file to attach.

4. The file will now be linked to the Trello card and can be opened directly.

This method reduces file duplication and ensures that everyone on the team is working with the most up-to-date version.

Summary: Making the Most of File Attachments in Trello

To summarize, attaching files and images in Trello is a powerful feature that improves productivity and collaboration. By keeping all project-related documents in one place, teams can work more efficiently, stay organized, and ensure easy access to critical information.

✅ Easy File Uploads – Attach documents from your computer or cloud storage.
✅ Streamlined Collaboration – Share files directly with team members.
✅ Organized File Management – Use naming conventions and delete outdated files.
✅ Cloud Integration – Link to Google Drive, Dropbox, and OneDrive for real-time updates.
✅ Enhanced Visuals – Use images to track progress and improve communication.

By implementing these best practices, individual users and teams can optimize their workflow and increase efficiency using Trello's file attachment features.

Next Steps

Now that you've learned how to **attach files and images to Trello cards**, let's move on to the next section:

📌 **3.2.2 Adding External Links to Cards** – Learn how to link to external resources like websites, documents, and online tools.

Stay tuned to further enhance your **Trello experience!** 🚀

3.2.2 Adding External Links to Cards

Trello is a versatile task management tool that enables users to centralize information, streamline workflows, and enhance team collaboration. One of the most powerful features of Trello is its ability to attach external links to cards, providing quick access to important online resources, project documents, reference materials, and integrated tools.

In this section, we will explore how to add, manage, and optimize external links in Trello cards. We will cover the step-by-step process of inserting links, discuss different types of links, explore real-world use cases, and highlight best practices to maximize efficiency.

Why Add External Links to Trello Cards?

Trello cards act as centralized information hubs where team members can find all necessary details about a task or project. Adding external links can:

✓ Enhance accessibility – Provide instant access to important resources without switching between apps.
✓ Improve workflow efficiency – Reduce time spent searching for documents, reports, or websites.
✓ Facilitate collaboration – Ensure team members are aligned by linking to shared files, instructions, or reference materials.
✓ Integrate with external tools – Connect Trello with project management apps, cloud storage, and communication platforms.

By strategically using external links, teams can keep their Trello boards organized, informative, and highly functional.

How to Add External Links to Trello Cards

Trello makes it incredibly simple to attach links to a card. Follow these steps to add an external link:

Method 1: Adding a Link in the Card Description

1. Open a Trello card where you want to add a link.

2. Click on the "Description" field to edit.

3. Paste the link directly into the description box.

4. Click "Save" to confirm.

◆ *Tip:* Trello automatically detects and converts URLs into clickable hyperlinks.

Method 2: Attaching a Link as an Attachment

1. Open a card and scroll down to the "Attachments" section.

2. Click "Attach a file" → Select "Attach a link".

3. Paste the URL and give it a meaningful title (optional).

4. Click "Attach" to finalize.

◆ *Tip:* If the link is from platforms like Google Drive, Dropbox, or OneDrive, Trello may generate a preview of the document.

Method 3: Adding Links in Comments

1. Open the **Trello card**.

2. Scroll to the **Comments** section.

3. **Type a message** and paste the link.

4. Click **"Send"** (or press Enter).

◆ *Tip:* Use @mentions to notify specific team members about the link.

Types of Links You Can Add to Trello Cards

∞ Project Management and Collaboration Tools

- Google Docs, Sheets, Slides – Link to shared documents, spreadsheets, and presentations.

- Microsoft OneDrive, SharePoint – Attach business reports and project files.

- Notion, Confluence, Evernote – Add links to knowledge bases and meeting notes.

💼 Cloud Storage and File Management

- Dropbox, Google Drive, Box – Store and access team files directly from Trello.

- GitHub, Bitbucket – Link to repositories for development teams.

▦ Calendars and Scheduling Tools

- Google Calendar, Outlook Calendar – Share meeting schedules and deadlines.
- Calendly, Doodle – Provide easy access to scheduling links.

▢▢ Workflow Automation and Integrations

- Zapier, IFTTT – Automate Trello workflows with integrated services.
- Slack, Microsoft Teams – Directly link conversations or channels for reference.

■ Reference Materials and Websites

- Industry blogs, articles, whitepapers – Share research materials.
- Online courses, YouTube tutorials – Link to learning resources.

By categorizing links **strategically**, users can ensure a well-structured workflow.

Best Practices for Managing External Links in Trello

To ensure external links enhance productivity instead of creating clutter, consider the following **best practices**:

1⃞ Use Clear and Descriptive Titles

◆ Instead of a generic link like:
https://docs.google.com/spreadsheets/d/xyz

✓ Use a clear, descriptive title:
🚀 "Project Budget – Q1 2025"

2⃞ Organize Links in a Logical Order

- Add important links at the top of the card description.
- Use bullet points for readability.

3⃞ Remove Outdated or Irrelevant Links

- Regularly review and **update links** to keep information accurate.

- Remove links to outdated documents to avoid confusion.

4⬜ Use Shortened URLs if Necessary

If a link is too long, consider using services like Bit.ly or TinyURL to create a short, clean link.

5⬜ Maintain Link Consistency Across Boards

- Establish a standard linking format within your team.

- Ensure everyone follows consistent naming conventions for documents and links.

By implementing these best practices, teams can ensure Trello remains a well-organized and efficient tool.

Real-World Use Cases for Adding Links in Trello

✅ Marketing Team Managing Campaigns

A marketing team uses Trello to track social media content. Each card represents a campaign and includes:

- A link to the Google Drive folder containing campaign assets.

- A Google Doc with the campaign strategy.

- A Calendly link for scheduling meetings with influencers.

✅ Software Development Team Managing Sprints

A development team tracks tasks in Trello with:

- Links to GitHub repositories for code review.

- A Jira ticket link for bug tracking.

- A Slack channel link for team discussions.

✅ HR Team Handling Employee Onboarding

HR professionals create a Trello board for onboarding new employees, adding:

- A Google Doc link to the employee handbook.

- A YouTube tutorial link on company policies.

- A Google Calendar link for orientation sessions.

These use cases show how strategically adding links enhances team productivity.

Summary: The Power of External Links in Trello

Adding external links to Trello cards is a simple yet powerful way to connect relevant information, enhance collaboration, and streamline workflows.

Key Takeaways

✓ Multiple ways to add links – in descriptions, attachments, or comments.
✓ Links improve accessibility – providing quick access to critical resources.
✓ Organizing links effectively boosts productivity.
✓ Best practices prevent clutter and ensure efficiency.
✓ Real-world applications showcase the impact of external links.

By following these guidelines, you can fully leverage external links in Trello to create a more connected, structured, and efficient workspace.

🚀 **Up Next:** In the next section, we will explore how to use **comments and mentions in Trello** to boost communication and collaboration within teams. Stay tuned!

3.3 Using Comments and Mentions for Collaboration

3.3.1 Commenting on Cards

Collaboration is at the heart of Trello, and one of its most effective tools for team communication is the commenting feature on Trello cards. Comments allow team members to discuss tasks, share updates, provide feedback, and track decisions—ensuring that important information is stored in one place rather than getting lost in emails or chat messages.

In this section, we will explore why commenting is essential in Trello, how to effectively use comments, best practices for keeping discussions organized, and real-world scenarios where commenting enhances productivity.

Why Commenting on Trello Cards is Important

In traditional task management methods, team discussions often happen over email chains, instant messaging, or even in-person meetings. While these methods have their place, they can lead to scattered information, missed details, and inefficient communication. Trello's commenting system solves these issues by providing a centralized, real-time conversation space directly on each task card.

Key Benefits of Using Comments in Trello

- 🖋 **Keeps all relevant discussions in one place** – No more searching emails or chat histories for important details.

- 🚀 **Enhances real-time collaboration** – Comments update instantly, keeping team members informed.

- 📌 **Provides context for tasks** – Instead of sending a separate message, comments remain attached to the task for easy reference.

- 🎯 **Improves accountability** – Team members can respond to updates and clarify responsibilities.

- 🔍 **Creates a historical record of discussions** – Even after a project is completed, comments serve as a reference point for decisions made.

By leveraging Trello's commenting feature, teams can improve communication efficiency, reduce misunderstandings, and streamline workflows.

How to Add Comments to Trello Cards

Adding a comment to a Trello card is simple and intuitive. Follow these steps to post your first comment:

1. **Open the Card** – Navigate to the Trello board, find the task card where you want to leave a comment, and click on it to open the **card details view**.

2. **Locate the Comment Box** – Scroll down to the "Activity" section where you'll see a text box labeled **"Write a comment..."**.

3. **Type Your Comment** – Enter your message, update, or feedback in the text field.

4. **Post the Comment** – Click the **"Send" button** (or press **Enter**) to submit your comment. It will now be visible to all team members who have access to the board.

💡 *Pro Tip:* You can use the **Shift + Enter** shortcut to create a **new line** within your comment instead of immediately posting it.

Formatting Your Comments for Clarity

Trello supports **basic formatting** to make comments more readable and structured. You can format your text using the following techniques:

- **Bold**: Use double asterisks (**bold**) to emphasize important points → **bold**

- *Italic*: Use a single asterisk (*italic*) for emphasis → *italic*

- Code formatting: Use backticks () to highlight code snippets → example`

- Lists: Use - or * to create bullet points

- @Mentions: Mention team members using @username to get their attention (covered in the next section)

Example of a Well-Formatted Comment:

Project Update:

- *Task completed:* Initial draft of the report is ready.

- **Next Steps:** Need feedback from @JohnDoe before moving to the final version.

- Deadline: March 30, 2025.

Using formatting ensures that your comments remain structured, readable, and easy to understand.

Best Practices for Effective Commenting

While commenting in Trello is simple, using it **effectively** requires some best practices to keep communication clear and efficient.

✅ 1. Keep Comments Concise and Actionable

Avoid long, cluttered messages that are difficult to read. Instead, make comments:

- Clear and direct: "@Emily Can you review this by Friday?"

- Action-oriented: "The final version is uploaded. @Team, please provide feedback."

⬤ *Avoid:* "Hey guys, I think this is done, but maybe we should check again? Let me know what you think."

✅ *Better:* "Task completed. @Mike, can you verify and approve?"

✅ 2. Use Mentions to Direct Comments to the Right People

Tagging the right people in your comments ensures they receive a notification and can respond promptly.

- Use @username to mention specific team members (e.g., @Sarah Can you check the budget report?)

- Mention @board or @card to notify everyone on the board or card.

💡 *Pro Tip:* If you don't tag someone, they might not see the comment immediately, leading to delays.

✅ 3. Provide Context in Your Comments

When commenting, give enough **context** so that others understand what you're referring to.

● *Avoid:* "Fixed it. Please check."

✓ *Better:* "@David, I fixed the formatting issues on the marketing report card. Please review and confirm."

✓ 4. Use Emojis for Quick Visual Cues

Sometimes, a simple emoji can make your message clearer.

- ✓ Checkmark for completed tasks → "Task is done ✓"

- 🔥 Urgent issues → "@Anna, we need this fixed ASAP 🔥"

- 💡 Ideas → "@Team, I have a suggestion 💡"

Emojis can enhance communication without making messages too lengthy.

✓ 5. Avoid Overloading with Too Many Comments

While Trello comments are useful, too many messages can become overwhelming.

- Instead of posting multiple short comments, consolidate your thoughts into one well-structured message.

- Use edits instead of new comments if you need to update your message.

● *Avoid:*

1. "I finished the first part."

2. "Actually, I just realized something needs changing."

3. "Ok, fixed it now."

✓ *Better:*

"@Jessica, I finished the first part and made some updates. Please review and let me know if you need changes."

Real-World Scenarios for Using Comments Effectively

To illustrate the power of Trello comments, let's look at some real-world use cases:

🚀 Project Management:

- Assigning tasks: "@Mike, can you take care of the client follow-up?"

- Reviewing work: "@Sara, I've uploaded the report. Let me know if it needs any changes."

📝 Content Creation:

- Drafting and approval process: "@Emma, the blog draft is ready. Please review and approve."

- Adding feedback: "I think we should change the intro to make it more engaging."

🔧 IT and Development Teams:

- Bug tracking: "@Devs, I found a UI glitch on the login page. Can we fix this?"

- Code updates: "@John, I pushed the latest update to GitHub. Please review."

Using comments in these ways ensures clear, effective, and productive team collaboration.

Final Thoughts

Trello's commenting feature is an essential tool for collaboration, enabling teams to communicate efficiently, provide feedback, and keep all relevant discussions in one place. By following best practices like keeping messages concise, tagging the right people, providing context, and using formatting effectively, teams can streamline workflows and improve productivity.

In the next section, we will explore how to use mentions (@) to improve collaboration even further! 🚀

3.3.2 Tagging Team Members

Collaboration is at the heart of Trello, and tagging team members using the mention feature (@username) is one of the most effective ways to enhance communication. Whether you need to assign a task, request feedback, notify a teammate of an update, or ask a question, using @mentions ensures that your message is seen by the right person at the right time.

This section will explore how to use mentions effectively, when and why to tag teammates, best practices for improving communication, and common mistakes to avoid when tagging team members in Trello.

What Is Tagging in Trello?

Tagging in Trello involves mentioning a specific team member using the "@" symbol followed by their username within a card comment, checklist, or description. When a user is tagged, they receive a notification, ensuring that they are aware of the message and can take necessary action.

Example of a mention in Trello:
"@JohnDoe Could you review this document and provide feedback by tomorrow? Thanks!"

Once a user is tagged, Trello will send a notification via email, mobile, and the Trello app, depending on their notification settings.

Why Tagging Team Members Is Important?

Tagging team members serves multiple purposes and is an essential collaboration tool in Trello. Here's why it matters:

✅ Ensures Team Members Stay Informed

- Trello boards can become crowded with multiple tasks, updates, and discussions. Tagging the right person ensures that critical updates don't get lost.

- *Example*: If a team leader needs approval on a design, tagging the designer and the manager ensures both parties see the message promptly.

✅ Clarifies Task Ownership

- Assigning cards to team members is helpful, but tagging them in specific discussions adds more clarity.

- *Example*: Instead of assuming someone will notice a deadline change, tagging them in a comment eliminates ambiguity.

✅ Reduces Email Overload

- Instead of relying on lengthy email threads, tagging keeps conversations centralized within Trello cards, making it easy to track discussions.

- *Example:* Instead of sending a separate email, tagging "@MarketingTeam" in a Trello card streamlines communication.

✅ Speeds Up Decision-Making

- Immediate notifications ensure quick responses, especially in time-sensitive situations.

- *Example:* If a last-minute change needs approval, tagging the manager speeds up the process.

✅ Encourages Team Collaboration

- Tagging helps different departments work together by bringing the right people into discussions at the right time.

- *Example:* A project manager can tag both the development and design teams when a new product feature is ready for review.

By leveraging tagging effectively, teams can enhance efficiency, reduce misunderstandings, and maintain seamless communication.

How to Tag Team Members in Trello

Tagging team members in Trello is straightforward and can be done in several places:

1. Tagging in Comments

The most common way to tag someone is within **a card comment**:

1. Open the Trello card.

2. Navigate to the **"Comments" section** at the bottom.

3. Type "@" followed by the person's username (e.g., @JohnDoe).

4. Enter your message and click **"Save"** or press **Enter**.

Example:

"@Sarah Can you update the project status by the end of today? Thanks!"

Once posted, the tagged user will receive a notification via email or Trello alerts, depending on their preferences.

2. Tagging in Checklists

- While checklists don't support direct tagging, you can mention a team member in a comment linked to the checklist.

- Example: If you create a checklist item "Submit Budget Report," you can comment "@FinanceTeam Please complete this checklist item by Friday."

3. Tagging in Card Descriptions

- You can mention a team member within the card description to highlight responsibilities or key notes.

- **Example:**
  ✦ *"@MarketingTeam Please update the campaign details in this card before the review meeting on Monday."*

4. Tagging Multiple Team Members at Once

- Trello allows you to tag multiple users in a single comment.

- **Example:**
  "@John @Emma @Michael Please review this document and add your feedback before Friday."

Best Practices for Tagging Team Members

To ensure effective communication, here are some best practices to follow when tagging teammates in Trello:

🏆 1. Tag Only When Necessary

- Avoid over-tagging users, as excessive notifications can become annoying and ignored.

- *Example:* Instead of tagging every team member, tag only those directly involved in a specific task.

🏆 2. Be Clear and Concise

- When tagging someone, specify what action you need from them.

- *Example:*
  ✗ *"@Lisa Check this out."* (Too vague)
  ✓ *"@Lisa Can you update the budget figures in this card by EOD?"* (Clear and actionable)

🏆 3. Use Group Mentions for Team-Wide Announcements

- If you're addressing an entire team, consider creating a team mention in the description or card.

- *Example:*
  "@DesignTeam Please finalize the homepage layout by next week."

🏆 4. Avoid Unnecessary Urgency

- If something is urgent, mark it properly with [URGENT] or a deadline.

- *Example:*
  "@Sarah, please complete this update by noon tomorrow. Thanks!"

🏆 5. Check Notification Settings

- Ensure that team members have their notification settings enabled so they don't miss important mentions.

By following these best practices, tagging will become a powerful tool rather than an annoying distraction.

Common Mistakes to Avoid When Tagging

📖 1. Tagging Without Context

- Don't tag someone without explaining why they are being mentioned.

- Example of a bad mention: *"@David?"* (Confusing)

- Better version: *"@David Can you upload the updated report here?"* (Clear and direct)

📖 2. Tagging Too Many People Unnecessarily

- If you tag multiple users who don't need to be involved, it can cause confusion and slow down decision-making.

📖 3. Assuming a Tag Guarantees Immediate Action

- Tagging does not mean someone will take action immediately. Follow up if necessary!

📖 4. Using Tags Instead of Assigning Tasks

- If a task belongs to someone, it's better to assign the card to them instead of just tagging.

Conclusion: Mastering the Art of Tagging in Trello

Tagging is a powerful collaboration tool in Trello that enhances team communication, accountability, and efficiency. By using mentions strategically, teams can ensure that important updates reach the right people at the right time.

Key Takeaways

✓ Use @username to notify team members.
✓ Keep messages clear, actionable, and concise.
✓ Tag only when necessary to avoid notification fatigue.
✓ Follow up on tagged messages when required.

By mastering tagging best practices, your team will enjoy seamless collaboration and improved workflow efficiency in Trello.

Next Steps

Now that you've learned how to effectively use comments and mentions, let's move on to Chapter 4: Managing Teams and Collaboration in Trello, where we'll discuss how to create and manage Trello teams and assign roles and permissions for better teamwork. 🚀

CHAPTER IV
Managing Teams and Collaboration in Trello

4.1 Creating and Managing a Trello Team

4.1.1 Adding and Removing Team Members

Trello is a powerful collaboration tool that enables teams to work efficiently, track progress, and stay organized. Whether you're managing a small startup, a large corporation, or a remote team, Trello's team management features allow you to control who has access to different boards, assign responsibilities, and ensure smooth workflows.

In this section, we will cover how to add and remove team members in Trello, best practices for team collaboration, and how to ensure security and efficiency within your team environment.

---

1. Understanding Trello Teams and Their Benefits

Before diving into the process of adding and removing team members, it is essential to understand what a Trello team is and why it is beneficial.

A Trello team (now called "Workspaces" as of recent updates) is a shared space where multiple users can collaborate on multiple Trello boards within a single organization.

Key Benefits of Using Trello Teams:

✓ Centralized Board Management – All team members can access relevant boards within the workspace.
✓ Simplified User Management – Easily control who can view or edit boards.

✅ Enhanced Collaboration – Team members can communicate via comments, mentions, and notifications.

✅ Consistent Organization – Use labels, templates, and automation to maintain workflow consistency.

✅ Better Security & Permissions – Control access levels for different team members.

Trello teams are widely used in businesses, schools, non-profits, and personal projects where multiple users need access to shared Trello boards.

2. How to Add Team Members to a Trello Team

Adding new team members to a Trello workspace allows them to collaborate on projects, access relevant boards, and contribute to tasks. Here's a step-by-step guide on how to do it.

Step 1: Navigate to Your Trello Team (Workspace)

1. Log in to your Trello account at trello.com.

2. Click on the Workspaces tab in the left-hand menu.

3. Select the team (workspace) you want to manage.

Step 2: Open the Team Members Section

1. Once inside the workspace, click on "Members" in the left sidebar.

2. This will display the list of current team members and their roles.

Step 3: Invite New Members

1. Click on "Invite Members" (located at the top right).

2. Enter the email address or Trello username of the person you want to add.

3. Click "Send Invitation".

4. The invited user will receive an email notification and must accept the invite to join the team.

Alternative Method: Adding Members via Board Invitation

- You can also add users directly to a board, and they will automatically be added to the team.

- Open the board settings, click "Invite," and enter the user's email.

- The invited user will be added as a board member, and you can later upgrade them to a team member.

Managing Pending Invitations

- If a user has not accepted the invitation, you can resend the invite from the Members section.

- Unaccepted invitations will expire after a period, so ensure users check their emails.

3. Assigning Roles and Permissions

When adding team members, you should define their roles and permissions to ensure smooth collaboration.

Trello Team Member Roles:

- Admin – Full control over the team, including adding/removing members, changing settings, and managing billing.

- Normal Member – Can access and edit shared boards but cannot manage team settings.

- Observer (Read-Only) – Can view boards but cannot make any changes.

How to Change a Member's Role:

1. Go to **"Members"** in the team workspace.

2. Click on the member's name.

3. Select **"Change Role"** and choose **Admin, Member, or Observer**.

4. Changes will apply instantly.

◆ *Best Practice:* Assign Admin rights only to trusted team leaders to prevent accidental deletions or unwanted changes.

4. How to Remove Team Members from a Trello Team

There may be situations where you need to remove a team member, whether they are leaving the company, switching departments, or no longer require access to specific boards.

Step 1: Navigate to the Members Section

1. Open your Trello Workspace.
2. Click on "Members" in the left-hand menu.

Step 2: Select the Member to Remove

1. Find the user you want to remove.
2. Click on their profile.

Step 3: Remove the User

1. Click "Remove from Workspace" or "Remove from Board" (depending on access level).
2. Confirm the action.
3. The user will lose access to all team boards and settings.

Alternative: Removing a Member from a Specific Board

- If you only want to remove a member from one board but not the entire team, go to:

  - **Board Menu → Members → Remove Member**

★ *Note:* Removing a user from a board does not delete their previous contributions (comments, task assignments, or activity logs remain).

5. Best Practices for Managing Team Members in Trello

✓ Keep Your Team List Updated

- Regularly review team members and remove those who no longer need access.
- Limit Admin roles to prevent accidental changes.

✓ Use Private vs. Public Boards Wisely

- Public Boards – Anyone can view them (ideal for open-source projects).
- Private Boards – Only invited members can access them (recommended for confidential company data).

✓ Train New Members on Trello Usage

- Provide basic training or documentation for new users.
- Ensure members understand workflows, labels, and team rules.

✓ Utilize Trello's Security Features

- Use two-factor authentication (2FA) for enhanced security.
- Restrict sensitive board permissions to trusted team members.

6. Summary: Key Takeaways

✓ Adding Team Members:

- Go to **Workspaces → Members → Invite** and send an invitation.
- Assign appropriate roles (Admin, Member, Observer).

- Ensure members accept the invitation.

✓ **Managing Roles and Permissions:**

- *Admins* have full control.

- *Normal Members* can edit but not manage settings.

- *Observers* have read-only access.

✓ **Removing Members:**

- Go to *"Members"* and select *"Remove"*.

- Removing a member *does not erase their past contributions*.

✓ **Best Practices:**

- Regularly **update** the team list.

- Limit **Admin access**.

- Use **private boards** for confidential work.

- Train new team members on **Trello's features**.

Final Thoughts

Managing a Trello team effectively ensures that collaboration remains seamless, roles are well-defined, and project workflows run smoothly. By adding the right people, assigning clear permissions, and keeping your team structure organized, you can maximize efficiency and productivity in Trello.

In the next section, we will explore how to collaborate effectively using task assignments, notifications, and other teamwork features in Trello.

4.1.2 Assigning Roles and Permissions

Effective team collaboration in Trello requires clear role assignments and permissions to ensure that every member has the appropriate level of access. Whether you're managing a small team or a large organization, understanding how to assign roles and set permissions will help maintain control, improve productivity, and enhance security.

In this section, we'll cover:

✓ Types of user roles in Trello

✓ How to assign and manage roles

✓ Board-specific permissions and team settings

✓ Best practices for role management

By the end, you'll have a complete understanding of how to effectively structure your team's roles and permissions in Trello.

Understanding Trello User Roles

Trello provides different levels of user roles and permissions to help teams control access and collaboration.

User Roles in a Trello Team

Trello teams typically consist of the following roles:

1. **Admins** – Have full control over the team, boards, and settings.

2. **Normal Members** – Can collaborate on boards but have limited administrative access.

3. **Observers (Premium Feature)** – Can view and comment on boards but cannot make changes.

Each role serves a specific purpose, ensuring that team members have the right level of control and responsibility within Trello.

Assigning Roles and Managing Team Members

Assigning roles in Trello is a straightforward process. Follow these steps to manage your team effectively:

Step 1: Accessing the Team Settings

1. Navigate to the Trello homepage.

2. Click on your team/workspace name on the left sidebar.

3. Select "Settings" to manage team roles.

Step 2: Adding Team Members

To assign roles, you must first add members to your team:

1. Go to the Members tab in your team settings.

2. Click "Invite Members" and enter their email addresses.

3. Select "Send Invitation" – Once accepted, they will be added to the team.

Step 3: Assigning Roles

Once a member is added, you can assign them a role:

1. Locate the member's name in the list.

2. Click on their name to open the role selection menu.

3. Choose between Admin, Normal Member, or Observer (if you have a Premium plan).

This setup ensures that only the right people have control over team settings and boards.

Board-Specific Permissions

Trello not only manages team-wide roles but also allows specific permissions on individual boards.

Board Membership Levels

Each board has different types of members:

- Board Admins – Full control over the board (can add/remove members, change settings, delete the board).

- Board Members – Can create, move, and edit cards but cannot change board settings.

- Observers (Premium Feature) – Can view and comment on cards but cannot edit them.

To **assign board roles**:

1. Open the board and click **"Show Menu"**.

2. Select **"Members"** to see the list of users.

3. Click on a user's name and set their **board-specific role**.

This feature helps maintain structured collaboration, especially when working with external users or temporary contributors.

Managing Permissions for Sensitive Information

When handling confidential projects, it's essential to control who can access what.

Ways to Restrict Access

✅ Private Boards – Only invited members can view and edit.
✅ Workspace Visibility Settings – Control whether boards are public, private, or team-only.
✅ Limited Editing Rights – Assign Observers to prevent unwanted modifications.
✅ Disable Board Copying – Prevent members from duplicating sensitive data.

By customizing these permissions, you can ensure only authorized team members can view and edit crucial information.

Best Practices for Assigning Roles and Permissions

Here are some best practices to help you effectively manage roles and permissions in Trello:

✅ 1. Keep Admins to a Minimum

Too many Admins can create security risks. Limit Admin access to only essential team members.

✅ 2. Regularly Review Team Members

Periodically audit team roles to remove inactive users and update responsibilities.

✅ 3. Use Observers for External Stakeholders

For clients or partners who need visibility but shouldn't edit cards, use Observers.

✅ 4. Set Board-Specific Permissions

Not every team member needs access to all boards. Assign roles based on the specific project.

✅ 5. Enable Two-Factor Authentication (2FA)

For enhanced security, encourage team members to enable 2FA to protect their accounts.

Summary: Optimizing Team Roles in Trello

🎯 Key Takeaways:

✅ Trello offers Admins, Members, and Observers to control team collaboration.
✅ Admins manage team settings, while Members contribute to boards.
✅ Use Board-specific roles for more granular permissions.
✅ Protect sensitive data by restricting access to private boards.
✅ Follow best practices to ensure smooth team management and security.

Final Thoughts

By effectively assigning roles and managing permissions, you can ensure that your Trello workspace remains organized, secure, and collaborative.

Now that you understand how to manage team roles, let's move on to the next section: ☞ **4.2 Collaborating Effectively with Trello** 🚀

4.2 Collaborating Effectively with Trello

4.2.1 Assigning Tasks to Team Members

Effective collaboration is the key to success in any team-based environment, whether in a corporate setting, a remote work setup, or a personal project with multiple contributors. Trello provides a straightforward and efficient way to assign tasks, track responsibilities, and ensure accountability.

In this section, we will explore how to:

- Assign tasks to team members using Trello.

- Use best practices to manage task assignments.

- Optimize team efficiency through clear ownership and accountability.

By mastering these techniques, you will be able to streamline your workflow and maximize the productivity of your team.

Understanding Task Assignments in Trello

Trello operates on a Kanban-style workflow, where tasks are represented as cards within lists on a board. Assigning a task in Trello means associating a specific team member with a Trello card to indicate their responsibility.

Each card can contain various details, including:
✓ Task description
✓ Due dates
✓ Checklists
✓ Attachments
✓ Labels for categorization
✓ Comments and discussions

By assigning members to these cards, teams gain **clarity** on who is responsible for completing each task. This prevents confusion, reduces redundancy, and ensures tasks do not go unattended.

How to Assign a Task in Trello

Assigning tasks in Trello is simple and can be done in a few steps:

Step 1: Open the Trello Board

Navigate to the Trello board that contains the task you want to assign. Ensure that all relevant team members have access to this board.

Step 2: Select the Task Card

Locate the specific task card that needs to be assigned. Click on the card to open its detailed view.

Step 3: Click on "Members"

In the card view, you will see an option labeled **"Members"** on the right-hand side. Click on it to open the team member selection panel.

Step 4: Choose a Team Member

A list of all board members will appear. Click on the name of the person responsible for the task. Their profile picture or initials will now appear on the card.

Step 5: Save and Notify the Assignee

Once assigned, the selected team member will receive a **notification** informing them of their new task.

Step 6: Monitor Progress

Regularly review the board to ensure assigned tasks are being completed within the expected timeframe.

Best Practices for Assigning Tasks in Trello

Assigning tasks is not just about selecting a name—it's about ensuring clarity, responsibility, and efficiency. Below are some best practices:

1. Be Clear About Responsibilities

- When assigning a task, provide a clear and detailed description of what needs to be done.

- Use checklists for multi-step tasks.

- Specify due dates to create a sense of urgency.

2. Assign Tasks to the Right People

- Ensure tasks are assigned based on skill sets and availability.

- Avoid overloading a single team member while leaving others with fewer tasks.

3. Use Labels and Priorities

- Apply color-coded labels to indicate priority levels (e.g., Urgent, High, Medium, Low).

- This helps team members quickly identify important tasks.

4. Enable Notifications

- Encourage assignees to enable Trello notifications to receive updates when they are mentioned or assigned a new task.

5. Monitor Task Progress

- Regularly review assigned tasks using Trello's "Filter by Member" feature to see what each person is working on.

- Utilize Trello Reports or Power-Ups like "Dashcards" to track progress.

Advanced Techniques for Managing Task Assignments

Once you have mastered the basics of assigning tasks, you can take it further by incorporating advanced Trello features to enhance collaboration.

1. Assign Multiple Team Members to a Task

- Trello allows multiple members to be assigned to the same card.

- This is useful when a task requires collaboration between multiple people.

2. Use Checklists for Subtasks

- Instead of creating multiple cards, break complex tasks into smaller action items within a checklist.

- Assign checklist items to specific individuals if necessary.

3. Utilize Due Dates and Reminders

- Set due dates for each task and enable reminders to ensure deadlines are met.

- Trello's Calendar Power-Up allows you to view deadlines in a calendar format.

4. Automate Task Assignments with Butler

Trello's built-in automation tool, **Butler**, can help streamline task assignments. Some useful automations include:

- Automatically assigning a member when a card moves to a specific list (e.g., assigning the **QA team** when a task moves to "Testing").

- Sending automatic **reminders** when a task's due date is approaching.

- Assigning team members based on **keywords** in card titles.

Case Study: Trello in Action for Task Assignments

Let's look at an example of Trello task assignments in a real-world scenario:

Scenario: A **marketing team** is using Trello to manage content creation for a blog.

- The team creates a Trello board called "Content Calendar."
- Lists are organized as "Ideas" → "In Progress" → "Review" → "Published."
- Each blog post is represented as a card that moves across lists.
- Tasks are assigned as follows:
    - Writers are assigned when a blog post moves to the "In Progress" list.
    - Editors are assigned when a post moves to "Review."
    - Social Media Team is assigned when a post moves to "Published" to promote it.
- Labels are added to indicate content type (Article, Video, Case Study).

By following this system, the team ensures a smooth content production workflow, with clear responsibilities for every step.

Common Challenges and How to Overcome Them

Even with a great task assignment system, teams may face some challenges. Below are common issues and solutions:

Challenge	Solution
Tasks are not being completed on time	Set due dates and send reminders. Use Trello reports to track pending tasks.
Too many people are assigned to a single task	Clearly define roles and responsibilities. Use checklists instead of assigning multiple people to a card.
Team members forget their assigned tasks	Encourage enabling Trello notifications and weekly reviews.
Lack of task updates from team members	Require regular status updates using Trello comments.

Conclusion

Assigning tasks in Trello is a simple yet powerful feature that enhances team collaboration and productivity. By using best practices such as clear task descriptions, priority labels, notifications, and automation, teams can work more efficiently and stay organized.

In the next section, we will explore how to set up notifications in Trello to stay informed about important task updates. 🚀

4.2.2 Setting Notifications for Task Updates

Effective collaboration in Trello requires clear and timely communication. One of the best ways to stay updated on task progress, changes, and team activities is by setting up and managing notifications. Trello offers a range of notification options that help users stay informed without feeling overwhelmed by unnecessary alerts.

In this section, we'll explore the different types of Trello notifications, how to customize them for better productivity, best practices for managing alerts, and strategies to ensure your team stays on top of project updates efficiently.

Understanding Trello Notifications

Trello provides several types of notifications to help you track changes and stay up to date with your tasks. These notifications appear in different locations, including:

- In-app notifications – Shown within Trello's notification panel.

- Email notifications – Sent to your registered email address.

- Push notifications – Delivered via Trello's mobile app.

- Desktop notifications – Available when using the Trello web or desktop app.

Each type of notification serves a unique purpose, allowing you to choose the best way to stay informed.

Types of Trello Notifications

To effectively use Trello notifications, it's important to understand the different types available:

1. In-App Notifications

- Found in the bell icon at the top-right of Trello's interface.

- Displays updates when someone mentions you, adds you to a card, modifies a due date, or changes a task you're following.

- Allows you to mark notifications as read or unread.

- Clicking a notification takes you directly to the relevant Trello card.

2. Email Notifications

- Sent when you haven't seen an in-app notification within a certain time frame.

- Includes summaries of activity on boards and cards you're subscribed to.

- Can be configured to be immediate, periodic, or disabled to reduce inbox clutter.

3. Push Notifications (Mobile App)

- Sent to your phone or tablet if you have the Trello mobile app installed.

- Useful for receiving updates when you're away from your computer.

- Allows you to interact with tasks directly from your device.

4. Desktop Notifications

- Available when using Trello on a desktop browser or the Trello desktop app.

- Sends pop-up alerts when there are task updates, mentions, or due date changes.

- Requires browser permissions to be enabled.

By understanding these notification types, you can tailor your settings to stay informed without being overwhelmed.

Customizing Notification Settings in Trello

Trello offers various options to control and personalize notifications based on your preferences. Here's how you can configure them:

1. Adjusting Board and Card Notifications

- Click on a **card** to open it.

- Click the **"Watch"** option to receive updates about that card.

- To stop receiving notifications, **unwatch** the card.

- To enable notifications for an entire **board**, click the **"Show Menu"** button on the right panel and select **"More"** → **"Watch"**.

2. Managing Email Notifications

- Go to **"Settings"** by clicking on your profile picture in the top-right corner.

- Select **"Notifications"** and adjust email frequency:

    o **"Instant"** – Get an email immediately when there's an update.

    o **"Periodic"** – Receive a summary email of updates.

    o **"Disabled"** – Turn off email notifications.

3. Configuring Mobile Push Notifications

- Open the **Trello mobile app**.

- Tap on your profile picture and go to **Settings**.

- Enable or disable push notifications based on your preferences.

- Customize which events trigger a notification (e.g., card assignments, due date reminders).

4. Enabling Desktop Notifications

- If using Trello in a browser, enable desktop notifications by:

    o Clicking on **Settings** in Trello.

    o Selecting **"Enable Desktop Notifications"**.

    o Granting permission in your browser's pop-up request.

- If using the Trello desktop app, notifications are enabled by default.

By customizing these settings, you can filter out unnecessary alerts and focus on what matters most.

Best Practices for Managing Trello Notifications

1. Avoid Notification Overload

- Only watch relevant cards and boards to reduce unnecessary alerts.

- Unsubscribe from email notifications if you prefer mobile or in-app updates.

- Use Slack or Microsoft Teams integrations to consolidate notifications.

2. Use Mentions Effectively

- Use @mentions in comments to notify specific team members without alerting the entire board.

- Example:

  - "@John, can you review this by tomorrow?" – Only John gets notified.

  - "@team, the deadline is approaching!" – Everyone on the board gets notified.

3. Set Up Due Date Reminders

- Trello sends automatic reminders before a task's deadline.

- To customize this:

  - Click on a card, set a due date, and select when to receive a reminder (e.g., 1 day before, 1 hour before).

- This ensures you never miss a deadline.

4. Use Power-Ups for Advanced Notifications

- Trello offers Power-Ups (integrations) to enhance notifications:

  - Slack Power-Up – Sends Trello updates to Slack channels.

  - Email-to-Board Power-Up – Converts emails into Trello cards.

  - Calendar Power-Up – Syncs due dates with Google Calendar for additional reminders.

By following these best practices, you can make Trello notifications work for you, not against you.

Ensuring Team Productivity with Notifications

Why are notifications crucial for team productivity?

1. Improves communication – Team members receive real-time updates.

2. Increases accountability – Everyone knows what tasks they're responsible for.

3. Reduces missed deadlines – Due date reminders ensure tasks stay on track.

4. Minimizes unnecessary meetings – Quick updates via notifications replace status check-ins.

How to Make Notifications Work for Your Team

- Encourage team members to customize their settings to avoid notification fatigue.

- Use team discussions to decide which updates are truly important.

- Balance automation and manual notifications – Avoid spamming users with unnecessary alerts.

By implementing a structured notification system, teams can collaborate more effectively without information overload.

Summary: Mastering Trello Notifications

To recap, Trello notifications help users:

✓ Stay informed about task updates in real-time.

✓ Receive alerts via in-app, email, mobile, and desktop notifications.

✓ Customize settings to avoid unnecessary distractions.

✓ Use mentions and due date reminders effectively.

✓ Integrate with Slack, Calendar, and other Power-Ups for better workflow.

By setting up Trello notifications correctly, you ensure that tasks are completed on time, team members stay accountable, and productivity remains high.

🚀 Next up: Learn how to use Trello for remote team collaboration and managing multiple projects effectively!

4.3 Using Trello for Remote Work

4.3.1 Best Practices for Distributed Teams

Remote work has become the new normal for many businesses, requiring effective tools and strategies to keep teams connected, productive, and organized. Trello is one of the best tools available for managing distributed teams, as it provides a flexible, visual, and easy-to-use platform for collaboration.

In this section, we will explore best practices for using Trello to manage remote teams efficiently. This includes structuring your workflow, maintaining transparency, enhancing communication, automating processes, integrating with other tools, and ensuring team engagement.

Understanding the Challenges of Remote Teams

Before diving into best practices, it's important to understand the common challenges remote teams face:

- Lack of face-to-face communication → Can lead to misunderstandings and decreased collaboration.

- Time zone differences → Delays in responses and coordination issues.

- Task visibility → Without proper tools, team members might not know what others are working on.

- Accountability concerns → Harder to track progress and ensure task completion.

- Disorganized workflows → Without a structured system, work can become chaotic.

Trello helps solve these challenges by creating a structured, transparent, and efficient remote work environment.

1. Structuring Your Trello Workspace for Remote Teams

A well-organized Trello board is the foundation of an efficient remote team.

Set Up a Standard Board Structure

To ensure clarity and efficiency, **establish a consistent structure** across your Trello boards. A common layout includes:

- **Backlog** – Ideas and future tasks.
- **To Do** – Tasks that need to be completed.
- **In Progress** – Tasks currently being worked on.
- **Review/Approval** – Tasks awaiting review.
- **Done** – Completed tasks.

This Kanban-style structure makes it easy for team members to see the progress of tasks at a glance.

Use Templates for Recurring Workflows

Trello allows you to create and save board templates, making it easy to maintain consistency across projects.

- Standardized task cards for weekly reports, project updates, or customer requests.
- Checklist templates for onboarding new employees or launching a product.

This saves time and ensures all team members follow the same workflow.

2. Enhancing Task Visibility and Accountability

Remote teams must ensure that everyone knows their responsibilities and can easily track progress.

Assign Tasks to Team Members

- Every Trello card should have an assigned member so that responsibilities are clear.
- Use due dates to keep tasks on schedule.
- Mention specific members in the card description for added clarity.

Use Labels for Prioritization

- Urgent (Red) – Needs immediate action.

- High Priority (Orange) – Must be done soon.

- Medium Priority (Yellow) – Important but not urgent.

- Low Priority (Green) – Can be done later.

Labels help team members focus on **high-impact tasks** first.

Track Progress with Checklists

Break tasks into smaller steps using checklists inside Trello cards. Example:

✅ Draft the project outline
✅ Review and edit content
✅ Finalize and publish

This ensures clarity on what's done and what's left.

---

3. Improving Communication in Remote Teams

Since remote teams lack in-person discussions, Trello helps keep conversations organized and accessible.

Use Comments for Clear Discussions

Instead of using email, keep all task-related discussions inside Trello cards:

- Tag team members (@mention) to notify them.

- Post updates directly under the relevant task.

- Avoid long email threads and scattered chats.

Set Up Trello Notifications

- Enable email or mobile notifications for important updates.

- Use the "Watch" feature on important cards to stay informed.

- Set up Slack or Microsoft Teams integrations for instant alerts.

This keeps everyone updated without unnecessary interruptions.

4. Automating Workflows to Save Time

Trello's Butler automation helps reduce manual work and improve efficiency.

Examples of Automated Actions

- Move completed tasks to the "Done" list automatically.

- Send reminders when deadlines are approaching.

- Assign tasks based on labels (e.g., all "Urgent" tasks go to a priority board).

Automation helps keep processes running smoothly without extra effort.

5. Integrating Trello with Other Remote Work Tools

Trello integrates with various tools to enhance productivity.

Best Trello Integrations for Remote Teams

- Slack → Get Trello notifications in Slack for quick updates.

- Google Drive & Dropbox → Attach files directly to Trello cards.

- Zoom → Add meeting links inside Trello cards.

- Asana & Jira → Sync with other project management tools.

These integrations streamline communication and task management.

6. Encouraging Team Engagement and Motivation

Remote teams lack face-to-face interaction, so keeping team morale high is essential.

Celebrate Wins and Progress

- Create a "Shout-Out" board where team members recognize each other's efforts.

- Use a "Milestone" list to track major achievements.

- Highlight "Team Member of the Month" to reward good work.

Schedule Regular Check-Ins

- Weekly team meetings to review progress and challenges.

- One-on-one check-ins to ensure team members feel supported.

- Virtual social events like game nights or coffee chats to build relationships.

This strengthens team connection and prevents isolation.

7. Reviewing and Adapting Your Trello Workflow

Continuous improvement is key to successful remote team management.

Analyze Productivity Trends

- Use Trello's dashboard view to track task completion rates.

- Identify bottlenecks and adjust workflows accordingly.

- Gather team feedback to improve the Trello setup.

Hold Monthly Retrospectives

- What worked well?

- What challenges did we face?

- What can we improve?

Regular reviews help teams stay efficient and adaptable.

Final Thoughts: Making Trello Work for Your Remote Team

Trello is an invaluable tool for remote teams, offering clear task management, seamless collaboration, automation, and integrations.

✅ Structured workflows ensure clarity and organization.
✅ Task assignments and checklists improve accountability.
✅ Comments and notifications keep everyone informed.
✅ Automation reduces repetitive work.

✅ Integrations enhance productivity.

✅ Team engagement strategies foster motivation.

By implementing these best practices, your remote team will work more efficiently, stay connected, and achieve goals faster.

Up next, we'll explore how to manage multiple projects remotely using Trello! 🚀

4.3.2 Managing Multiple Projects Remotely

In today's digital work environment, managing multiple projects remotely has become an essential skill for teams and businesses. Trello, with its intuitive visual structure and powerful collaboration features, makes it easier for teams to keep track of various projects from anywhere in the world. However, handling multiple projects effectively requires strategic organization, clear communication, automation, and integration with other tools.

In this section, we will explore best practices for using Trello to manage multiple remote projects, including setting up structured workspaces, optimizing board layouts, using Power-Ups for efficiency, automating repetitive tasks, and integrating with essential project management tools.

Structuring Your Trello Workspace for Multiple Projects

When managing multiple projects, the first step is to create a well-organized Trello workspace that allows you to easily navigate between projects, track progress, and assign tasks efficiently.

Using Trello Workspaces for Organization

Trello offers Workspaces, which serve as a central hub for organizing multiple related boards. This feature is particularly useful for teams handling various projects simultaneously.

- Create a separate board for each project: This ensures clarity and prevents clutter within a single board.

- Group similar projects within a Workspace: For example, a marketing team might have a Workspace containing boards for content planning, social media campaigns, and email marketing.

- Use naming conventions to keep boards easily identifiable (e.g., "Q2 Product Launch – Development," "Q2 Product Launch – Marketing").

By structuring Trello effectively, team members can quickly switch between projects without losing focus.

Optimizing Board Layouts for Efficiency

Once you have your workspace set up, the next step is to structure your individual Trello boards for maximum efficiency.

Choosing the Right Board Structure

The way you set up your Trello boards depends on the complexity of your projects. Common board structures include:

- Traditional Kanban Workflow: Uses columns like To-Do, In Progress, Review, Done to track tasks across different stages.

- Project Phase Boards: Divides tasks into major project phases (e.g., Research, Development, Testing, Deployment).

- Departmental Boards: For organizations managing multiple projects across different teams (e.g., Sales, Engineering, HR).

Using Lists Effectively

Within each board, lists help structure workflows for each project. Here are some effective list structures:

1. By Task Status: To-Do | In Progress | Review | Done

2. By Timeframe: This Week | Next Week | Next Month | Completed

3. By Team Members: John's Tasks | Sarah's Tasks | Alex's Tasks

4. By Project Components: Design | Development | Marketing | Testing

By selecting the right structure, teams can maintain clarity and prevent bottlenecks in remote project management.

Assigning Tasks and Responsibilities Clearly

When working remotely, it is crucial to ensure accountability by assigning clear roles and responsibilities. Trello provides various ways to accomplish this.

Assigning Team Members to Cards

- Each Trello card represents a task, and assigning members ensures that everyone knows who is responsible for what.

- You can assign multiple people to a card if a task requires collaboration.

- Team members can use profile icons to quickly identify their tasks on a board.

Using Labels and Tags for Clarity

- Color-coded labels help categorize tasks by priority, project type, or department.

- Example: A marketing board might use labels like "Urgent," "Social Media," "Paid Ads," and "SEO."

- Filtering by labels allows team members to quickly view their relevant tasks.

Setting Due Dates and Deadlines

- Assigning due dates ensures that tasks stay on schedule.

- Trello sends automatic reminders when deadlines approach.

- Teams can use calendar view (via Trello Power-Ups) to track project timelines visually.

With clear assignments and structured workflows, teams can work remotely without confusion.

Leveraging Trello Power-Ups for Multi-Project Management

Trello **Power-Ups** (add-ons) expand Trello's functionality, making it easier to manage multiple projects efficiently. Some key Power-Ups include:

Calendar Power-Up

- Helps visualize deadlines across multiple projects.
- Syncs with Google Calendar, Outlook, and Apple Calendar.

Table View (Premium Feature)

- Provides a spreadsheet-like overview of tasks across multiple Trello boards.
- Helps teams track progress on multiple projects in one view.

Time Tracking Power-Ups

- Tools like Toggl, Harvest, and TimeCamp help track time spent on tasks.
- Useful for remote teams billing clients or tracking productivity.

Card Sync Power-Up

- Syncs cards across multiple Trello boards, ensuring updates are reflected everywhere.
- Helps when a task spans multiple projects.

Using Power-Ups helps automate and streamline project tracking, making it easier to manage remote work.

Automating Workflows with Butler

Trello's Butler automation tool reduces manual work and improves efficiency in managing multiple projects.

How Butler Automation Can Help

- Move tasks automatically based on due dates (e.g., move overdue tasks to a "High Priority" list).
- Auto-assign team members based on task type.
- Send automated notifications when a card is moved to a specific list.
- Create recurring tasks for ongoing projects.

Example Butler Automation

- "When a card is moved to 'In Progress,' assign it to the project manager."

- "When a card is due in 3 days, send a Slack reminder to the assigned member."

By automating repetitive tasks, teams can focus on strategic work rather than administrative tasks.

Integrating Trello with Other Productivity Tools

To manage multiple projects effectively, Trello integrates with various project management and communication tools.

Popular Integrations

- Slack – Receive Trello updates in Slack channels.

- Google Drive & Dropbox – Attach documents and files to Trello cards.

- Jira – Sync Trello with software development workflows.

- Asana & Monday.com – Connect Trello with other project management platforms.

Using these integrations ensures that teams can collaborate smoothly across different platforms.

Best Practices for Managing Multiple Projects Remotely

To wrap up, here are some best practices for handling multiple remote projects with Trello:

✅ Standardize workflows – Use consistent board structures for all projects.
✅ Ensure visibility – Use shared Workspaces and Power-Ups like Calendar View.
✅ Leverage automation – Use Butler to handle repetitive tasks.
✅ Encourage communication – Utilize comments, mentions, and Slack integration.
✅ Regularly review progress – Hold virtual check-ins and use reporting tools.

By following these best practices, teams can efficiently manage multiple projects in a remote work environment while staying organized, productive, and collaborative.

Final Thoughts

Managing multiple projects remotely can be challenging, but with Trello's flexible structure, automation features, and integrations, teams can work efficiently across different projects without feeling overwhelmed.

Now that you've learned how to handle multiple projects in Trello, you're ready to explore more advanced collaboration techniques to maximize your team's productivity.

🚀 Next, let's dive into advanced team collaboration techniques in Trello! 🎯

CHAPTER V
Automating Workflows with Trello

5.1 Introduction to Trello Automation

Why Automation Matters in Task Management

Managing tasks manually can be time-consuming and inefficient, especially when dealing with repetitive actions like assigning tasks, moving cards, or sending reminders. Automation eliminates repetitive work, reduces human errors, and ensures that workflows run smoothly without constant supervision.

Trello, while simple and intuitive, becomes even more powerful when you leverage its automation features. By automating workflows, users can focus on more critical tasks instead of spending time on routine updates.

In this chapter, we'll explore how Trello automation works, its benefits, and how you can leverage Butler, Trello's built-in automation tool, along with Power-Ups and integrations to streamline your work.

What is Trello Automation?

Trello automation refers to using rules, triggers, and integrations to handle repetitive tasks automatically. This can include:

✅ Automatically moving cards when a due date is reached.

✅ Assigning team members based on specific criteria.

✅ Sending reminders and notifications when tasks are overdue.

✅ Triggering emails or Slack messages when a card's status changes.

✅ Labeling and sorting tasks based on predefined rules.

Trello offers two primary ways to automate workflows:

- **Butler** – Trello's built-in automation tool that allows users to create rules, buttons, and scheduled commands.

- **Power-Ups & Integrations** – Third-party extensions that connect Trello with other applications like Slack, Google Drive, Zapier, and more.

Benefits of Automating Trello Workflows

Automation in Trello brings numerous benefits, whether you are managing personal tasks, team projects, or enterprise-level workflows.

1. Saves Time and Reduces Manual Work

Instead of manually updating tasks, automation handles routine actions, allowing you to focus on more valuable work. For example:

- Automatically moving tasks to "Completed" when checklists are finished.

- Assigning cards to team members based on labels or priorities.

- Sending email notifications to stakeholders when a project milestone is reached.

2. Improves Workflow Consistency

Automation ensures that tasks follow the same structured process every time. This is especially useful for:

- Onboarding new employees – Automatically assign training tasks.

- Customer support – Move tickets through different resolution stages.

- Content creation – Move blog posts from "Draft" to "Published" automatically.

3. Enhances Collaboration and Communication

Automation keeps teams informed without requiring constant manual updates. For example:

- Notify team members in Slack when a task is completed.

- Send an email reminder when a due date approaches.

- Automatically update a shared Google Sheet with task progress.

4. Reduces Errors and Ensures Accountability

By automating assignments and notifications, Trello reduces human errors, ensuring that no tasks get forgotten or lost.

- Automatically remind users about overdue tasks.
- Prevent tasks from being neglected or skipped.
- Assign the correct team members based on predefined criteria.

5. Increases Productivity and Efficiency

When repetitive tasks are automated, teams can work faster and more efficiently. Instead of spending time on manual updates, users can focus on high-priority work.

How Trello Automation Works

Trello automation is based on triggers, conditions, and actions.

- **Trigger** – What starts the automation (e.g., when a new card is added).
- **Condition** – A rule that must be met (e.g., if the card has a due date).
- **Action** – What happens as a result (e.g., assign a member, move the card).

Example 1: Automating Task Assignments

Scenario: You have a Trello board where tasks need to be assigned to different team members based on priority.

📌 **Automation Rule:**

- If a card is labeled **"Urgent"**, assign it to the **Project Manager**.
- If a card is labeled **"Technical"**, assign it to the **Developer**.
- If a card is labeled **"Design"**, assign it to the **Graphic Designer**.

✅ **Outcome:** Cards are assigned automatically, reducing manual work.

Example 2: Moving Cards When Tasks Are Completed

Scenario: You want tasks to move automatically to the "Completed" list when all checklist items are checked.

📌 **Automation Rule:**

- If a card's **checklist is 100% completed**, move it to the **"Completed"** list.

✅ **Outcome:** The workflow stays organized without manual dragging of tasks.

Overview of Trello's Automation Tools

Trello offers two main ways to automate workflows:

1. Butler (Built-in Automation)

Butler is Trello's native automation tool that allows users to create custom rules, buttons, and scheduled commands.

✅ **Key Features of Butler:**

- Rules – Automate actions when specific triggers occur (e.g., moving a card when due).

- Card Buttons – Custom buttons that perform multiple actions in one click.

- Board Buttons – Similar to card buttons but apply to the whole board.

- Scheduled Commands – Automate actions at specific times (e.g., every Monday at 9 AM).

2. Power-Ups and Third-Party Integrations

While Butler is built-in, Trello also allows external Power-Ups and integrations to enhance automation. Some popular ones include:

- Zapier – Connects Trello with 2,000+ apps like Google Sheets, Gmail, Slack, and Asana.

- Slack Power-Up – Sends automatic updates to Slack channels.

- Google Drive Power-Up – Attaches files automatically when a task is created.

- Calendar Power-Up – Syncs due dates with Google Calendar or Outlook.

📌 **Example:** If you receive an email in Gmail labeled "Project Update", Zapier can automatically create a Trello card for follow-up.

Getting Started with Trello Automation

Now that we understand the basics, here's how you can start using automation in Trello:

1️⃣ Identify repetitive tasks – What actions do you often do manually?
2️⃣ Set up Butler commands – Create rules and buttons to handle these tasks.
3️⃣ Enable Power-Ups – Connect Trello with other tools to enhance workflow.
4️⃣ Test your automations – Ensure they work as expected.
5️⃣ Refine and optimize – Make adjustments based on team feedback.

Summary: Why Automate in Trello?

To recap, Trello automation helps users:

✅ Save time by eliminating manual work.
✅ Ensure consistency by following structured workflows.
✅ Enhance team collaboration with automatic updates.
✅ Reduce errors by assigning tasks automatically.
✅ Boost efficiency by letting Trello handle repetitive actions.

In the next section, we'll dive deeper into Butler for task automation and explore how to set up automation rules to make your Trello boards work for you. 🚀

5.2 Using Butler for Task Automation

Trello's Butler automation tool is one of its most powerful features, allowing users to automate repetitive tasks, optimize workflows, and boost productivity. Instead of manually moving cards, assigning tasks, or updating due dates, Butler can handle these actions automatically based on predefined rules.

In this section, we will explore how Butler works, its key benefits, and the process of setting up automation rules to streamline your Trello workflow.

5.2.1 Setting Up Automation Rules

What Are Automation Rules in Butler?

Automation rules in Butler allow users to set conditions and trigger specific actions when those conditions are met. This eliminates the need for manual intervention and ensures that tasks progress smoothly.

For example, you can create a rule that:
✅ Moves a card to the "Done" list when a checklist is completed.
✅ Automatically assigns team members when a new card is created.
✅ Sends a notification when a task is overdue.

Setting up these rules saves time, reduces errors, and keeps workflows organized.

Step-by-Step Guide to Creating Automation Rules

Let's go through the process of setting up automation rules in Butler.

Step 1: Accessing Butler

1. Open Trello and navigate to the board where you want to set up automation.

2. Click on **"Automation"** from the **board menu** (located in the top-right corner).

3. Select **"Rules"** from the Butler automation menu.

Step 2: Understanding the Structure of an Automation Rule

Each Butler rule consists of **three key elements**:

1. **Trigger** – The condition that activates the automation (e.g., when a card is moved to a list).

2. **Action** – What happens when the trigger is met (e.g., assigning a member, moving the card).

3. **Optional Conditions** – Additional filters to refine when the rule applies.

For example:

- **Trigger**: "When a card is moved to the 'In Progress' list"

- **Action**: "Assign John Doe and set the due date to 3 days later"

Step 3: Creating a Basic Automation Rule

Let's set up a simple rule where a card moves to the "Done" list automatically when all tasks in its checklist are completed.

1. In the Butler **Rules** tab, click **"Create Rule"**.

2. Click **"Add Trigger"** → Select **"When a checklist is completed"**.

3. Click **"Add Action"** → Select **"Move the card to list"** → Choose **"Done"**.

4. Click **"Save"**.

Now, whenever all checklist items in a Trello card are marked as completed, the card will automatically move to the **"Done"** list.

Advanced Automation Rules in Butler

While basic rules are useful, Trello Butler allows advanced automation, including:

1. Automating Task Assignments

Instead of manually assigning team members, you can create a rule that assigns members based on keywords or specific actions.

✅ Example Rule:

- **Trigger**: "When a card is created in the 'To-Do' list"
- **Action**: "Assign @JohnDoe and set due date to 5 days later"

This ensures that new tasks are assigned to the right person without delay.

2. Auto-Moving Cards Based on Due Dates

You can set up a rule that moves overdue tasks to a special list for better tracking.

✅ Example Rule:

- **Trigger**: "When a card is overdue"
- **Action**: "Move the card to the 'Urgent' list and send a Slack notification"

This prevents important tasks from being forgotten.

3. Automating Labels and Priorities

You can create a rule to automatically add a high-priority label to urgent tasks.

✅ Example Rule:

- **Trigger**: "When a card is added to the 'Critical Tasks' list"
- **Action**: "Add a red 'Urgent' label and set the due date to 2 days later"

This helps in visually identifying urgent tasks.

4. Sending Automated Notifications

Butler can also send email or Slack notifications when key actions happen.

✅ Example Rule:

- **Trigger**: "When a due date is 24 hours away"
- **Action**: "Send an email reminder to assigned members"

This ensures that deadlines are never missed.

Best Practices for Using Butler Automation

While automation is powerful, it's important to set up rules strategically to avoid overwhelming the workflow. Here are some best practices:

✅ Start with simple rules – Automate only the most repetitive tasks first.
✅ Test your rules – Ensure that automations work as expected before applying them to large projects.
✅ Use filters wisely – Add conditions (e.g., only apply to certain lists or members) to avoid unnecessary triggers.
✅ Keep automation organized – Name your rules clearly so they are easy to manage.
✅ Monitor performance – Regularly check how automation is impacting your workflow and adjust as needed.

Final Thoughts on Butler Automation

By setting up smart automation rules in Trello, you can eliminate repetitive manual tasks, increase efficiency, and ensure smoother project management.

🏃 **What's next?** In the next section, we'll explore **how to extend Trello's capabilities using Power-Ups**! Stay tuned! 💡

5.2.2 Automating Task Assignments

Task assignments are a crucial aspect of any workflow, ensuring that responsibilities are clearly distributed among team members. However, manually assigning tasks can become time-consuming, especially in large projects with multiple moving parts. This is where Butler, Trello's built-in automation tool, can help. By leveraging Butler's automation capabilities, you can automatically assign tasks based on predefined rules, ensuring that work is delegated efficiently with minimal effort.

In this section, we'll explore how Butler can automate task assignments, improve workflow efficiency, and reduce manual workload. We'll cover why automated assignments are useful, how to create rules for automatic assignments, different use cases for task automation, and best practices to ensure smooth implementation.

Why Automate Task Assignments?

Manual task assignment works well for small teams or simple projects, but as projects grow in complexity, automating the assignment process brings several key benefits:

- **Saves time**: Eliminates the need to manually assign tasks every time a new card is created.

- **Reduces human error**: Ensures that tasks are always assigned correctly, avoiding miscommunication.

- **Ensures accountability**: Assigns tasks to the right people immediately, keeping projects on track.

- **Improves workflow efficiency**: Streamlines task delegation, ensuring work is evenly distributed.

- **Enhances collaboration**: Everyone knows their responsibilities without needing extra instructions.

By automating task assignments with Butler, you **free up valuable time** for more important work and create a **smoother, more efficient workflow**.

Setting Up Automated Task Assignments with Butler

To start automating task assignments in Trello, you'll need to create custom rules using Butler. Butler allows you to define triggers (events that activate the automation) and actions (what happens when the rule is triggered).

Step 1: Accessing Butler in Trello

1. Open your Trello board.

2. Click on **Automation** in the top menu.

3. Select the **Rules** tab (this allows you to create task assignment rules).

Step 2: Defining the Automation Rule

Now, you'll need to create a rule that automatically assigns tasks when specific conditions are met. Here are some common examples:

1. Assign a task when a card is created in a list

If you have a **"To-Do"** list where all new tasks start, you can set up an automation rule so that tasks in this list are automatically assigned to a specific team member.

Example Rule:

- **Trigger**: When a card is added to the **"To-Do"** list
- **Action**: Assign the task to **John Doe**

How to Set It Up:

1. In the **Rules** tab, click **Create a Rule**.
2. Under **Trigger**, select **When a card is added to list "To-Do"**.
3. Under **Actions**, select **Assign the card to John Doe**.
4. Click **Save Rule**.

✓ Now, every time a card is added to the **"To-Do"** list, John Doe will automatically be assigned.

2. Assign tasks based on card labels

You can assign tasks based on **labels** (e.g., "Urgent", "Marketing", "Development"). This ensures that different types of tasks go to the right team members.

Example Rule:

- **Trigger**: When a card is labeled **"Marketing"**
- **Action**: Assign the card to **Sarah Smith** (Marketing Lead)

How to Set It Up:

1. In **Butler**, create a new rule.
2. Under **Trigger**, select **When a label "Marketing" is added to a card**.
3. Under **Actions**, select **Assign the card to Sarah Smith**.
4. Click **Save Rule**.

✅ Now, every time a card is tagged as **"Marketing"**, it will be automatically assigned to Sarah.

3. Assign tasks based on due dates

If you have recurring tasks with **tight deadlines**, Butler can automatically assign them to the right person when the due date approaches.

Example Rule:

- **Trigger**: When a card **due in 3 days**
- **Action**: Assign the card to **Project Manager**

How to Set It Up:

1. In Butler, create a rule.
2. Under **Trigger**, select **When a card is due in 3 days**.
3. Under **Actions**, select **Assign the card to Project Manager**.
4. Click **Save Rule**.

✅ Now, **tasks due in 3 days** will automatically be assigned, ensuring nothing is overlooked.

4. Assign tasks when a checklist item is completed

If a task requires multiple steps, you can assign the next person automatically when a **checklist item** is marked as complete.

Example Rule:

- **Trigger**: When checklist item **"Research complete"** is checked off
- **Action**: Assign the card to **Content Writer**

✅ This ensures that once **one stage** is complete, the next person is immediately assigned to continue the work.

Use Cases for Automated Task Assignments

Butler's automation is highly versatile and can be used across different workflows:

- Project Management: Assign project managers when new milestones are created.

- Content Creation: Assign blog writers when an article idea is added to the board.

- Customer Support: Assign support tickets to the next available team member.

- Software Development: Assign developers based on feature requests.

- Personal Productivity: Auto-assign tasks to yourself when you create new cards.

No matter the industry, task automation saves time and ensures that no work gets overlooked.

Best Practices for Automating Task Assignments

To get the most out of automated assignments, follow these best practices:

☑ Start with simple rules – Avoid overly complex automation at the beginning.
☑ Use clear labels – Ensure labels are well-defined so Butler can assign tasks correctly.
☑ Regularly review automation rules – Update rules to match changing workflows.
☑ Avoid over-automation – Keep human oversight to ensure quality.
☑ Test your automation – Run trial tasks to confirm that rules work as expected.

By following these best practices, you maximize efficiency without losing control over your workflow.

Conclusion: Enhancing Productivity with Automated Assignments

Automating task assignments in Trello using Butler is a game-changer for productivity. It ensures that tasks are assigned quickly, responsibilities are clear, and workflows run smoothly without constant manual intervention.

With automation, you reduce errors, save time, and ensure every team member stays on top of their responsibilities. Whether you're a freelancer, team leader, or project manager, using Butler for task assignments will help you work smarter, not harder.

Now that you understand how to automate task assignments, in the next section, we'll explore how Power-Ups can further extend Trello's capabilities. 🚀

5.3 Power-Ups: Extending Trello's Capabilities

Trello is a powerful and flexible tool on its own, but its true potential is unlocked with Power-Ups. Power-Ups are integrations and add-ons that extend Trello's functionality, allowing users to customize their workflow, streamline repetitive tasks, and integrate with other productivity tools.

Whether you need advanced reporting, automation, file management, or enhanced collaboration, Trello Power-Ups can transform your boards into a highly efficient workspace.

In this section, we will explore how Power-Ups work, their benefits, and some of the most popular Power-Ups for increasing productivity.

5.3.1 Popular Power-Ups for Productivity

There are hundreds of Power-Ups available in Trello's marketplace, but not all of them are necessary for every workflow. Below, we will cover some of the most widely used Power-Ups that help boost efficiency in task management, communication, reporting, and automation.

1. Calendar Power-Up: Visualizing Deadlines and Schedules

Overview

The Calendar Power-Up is one of the most essential productivity enhancements in Trello. It allows users to view cards with due dates in a calendar format, making it easier to manage schedules, plan projects, and track deadlines.

Key Features

✅ Switch between weekly and monthly views to get a clear picture of upcoming tasks.
✅ Drag and drop cards within the calendar to reschedule tasks effortlessly.
✅ Sync Trello deadlines with Google Calendar, Outlook, and Apple Calendar.
✅ Filter calendar views based on labels, members, or lists.

Best Use Cases

▦ Project Management: Track deadlines and upcoming tasks.
✒ Content Planning: Organize blog posts, social media schedules, or marketing campaigns.
⌖ Event Planning: Schedule events, meetings, and deadlines in an organized calendar view.

2. Custom Fields: Adding More Information to Cards

Overview

The Custom Fields Power-Up lets users add additional fields to Trello cards beyond the default title, description, and due date. This is particularly useful for tracking specific details that standard Trello cards don't support.

Key Features

✓ Add drop-down menus, checkboxes, text fields, number fields, and dates to cards.
✓ Color-code and categorize tasks more effectively.
✓ Display important card details without opening the card.
✓ Improve organization and streamline team collaboration.

Best Use Cases

📌 Task Prioritization: Add priority levels (e.g., High, Medium, Low) for better task management.
☐ Bug Tracking: Assign severity levels, version numbers, or statuses.
💰 Expense Tracking: Use number fields to monitor costs, budgets, or invoices.

3. Google Drive Power-Up: Seamless File Management

Overview

The Google Drive Power-Up integrates Trello with Google Drive, allowing users to attach documents, spreadsheets, and presentations directly to Trello cards.

Key Features

✅ Attach Google Docs, Sheets, Slides, and PDFs to cards with a single click.

✅ View document previews without leaving Trello.

✅ Automatically update files when changes are made in Google Drive.

✅ Search Google Drive files directly from Trello.

Best Use Cases

📁 **Team Collaboration**: Share important project files without searching through emails.

📘 **Documentation Management**: Link training manuals, SOPs, and reference materials.

📊 **Reporting**: Store and update spreadsheets containing key project data.

4. Slack Power-Up: Enhancing Team Communication

Overview

The **Slack Power-Up** connects Trello with Slack, enabling seamless communication between teams by sending updates, reminders, and notifications about Trello activity directly to Slack channels.

Key Features

✅ Create Trello cards directly from Slack messages.

✅ Receive real-time notifications in Slack when tasks are updated.

✅ Automatically send Trello updates to a specific Slack channel.

✅ Mention team members in Slack and link them to specific Trello cards.

Best Use Cases

💬 **Team Coordination**: Ensure everyone stays updated on task progress.

🏃 **Project Management**: Quickly assign tasks and follow up via Slack.

⚡ **Reducing Email Clutter**: Replace lengthy email threads with instant Trello updates in Slack.

5. Butler Power-Up: Automating Repetitive Tasks

Overview

Butler is Trello's built-in automation tool that helps users automate repetitive tasks and create workflows without writing a single line of code.

Key Features

✅ Set up **rules** to automatically move cards when certain conditions are met.

✅ Create **custom buttons** to trigger multiple actions at once.

✅ Schedule **recurring tasks** like weekly reports or check-ins.

✅ Automate task assignments based on due dates or workflow stages.

Best Use Cases

☐ **Task Delegation**: Automatically assign team members when a card moves to a specific list.

▦ **Deadline Reminders**: Move overdue tasks to a high-priority list.

🚀 **Efficiency Boost**: Automate repetitive manual tasks to save time.

---

6. Time Tracking with Trello: Boosting Productivity Metrics

Overview

Tracking time spent on tasks is critical for productivity analysis, billing, and project estimation. Power-Ups like Toggl Track, Clockify, and Harvest allow users to track time directly within Trello.

Key Features

✅ Start/stop timers directly from Trello cards.

✅ Generate reports on time spent per task or project.

✅ Track billable hours for freelancers and agencies.

✅ Identify bottlenecks and optimize workflows.

Best Use Cases

☐ **Freelancers & Consultants**: Track billable hours for client projects.

▥ **Project Managers**: Monitor time spent on tasks to improve efficiency.

💼 **HR & Payroll**: Log employee working hours for payroll processing.

Summary: How Power-Ups Transform Trello

Power-Ups significantly enhance Trello's capabilities by adding new functionalities, improving collaboration, and streamlining workflows. Whether you need better organization, automation, or integration with third-party tools, there's a Power-Up that can help.

✓ **Calendar Power-Up** – Perfect for visualizing deadlines and schedules.
✓ **Custom Fields** – Adds extra details to cards for better task tracking.
✓ **Google Drive Integration** – Keeps all important documents easily accessible.
✓ **Slack Integration** – Improves team communication and coordination.
✓ **Butler Automation** – Eliminates repetitive manual work.
✓ **Time Tracking** – Helps measure productivity and manage work hours efficiently.

By strategically using Power-Ups, teams can customize Trello to fit their unique workflow, making project management smoother and more efficient.

Next Steps: Optimizing Your Workflow

Now that you understand how Power-Ups can enhance Trello's capabilities, the next step is to explore how to use Trello's advanced features and best practices to maximize efficiency.

In the next chapter, we'll dive into advanced Trello tips, organizing your boards for efficiency, and best practices for different use cases. 🚀

5.3.2 Integrating Trello with Other Tools (Google Drive, Slack, etc.)

Trello is a powerful standalone tool, but its true potential is unlocked when integrated with other productivity apps and services. Whether you need better file management, communication, reporting, or automation, Trello Power-Ups provide seamless connections to the tools you already use.

This section explores why integrating Trello with other tools is beneficial, which integrations are most valuable, and how to set them up for an optimized workflow.

Why Integrate Trello with Other Tools?

While Trello is excellent for task and project management, no tool can do everything on its own. That's where integrations come in. By connecting Trello to cloud storage, messaging platforms, reporting tools, and automation services, you can:

✅ **Centralize work** – Keep everything in one place without constantly switching between apps.

✅ **Boost collaboration** – Enhance teamwork with real-time updates and shared resources.

✅ **Improve efficiency** – Automate repetitive tasks and reduce manual effort.

✅ **Enhance visibility** – Get better tracking, reporting, and insights across multiple tools.

Let's explore some of the most powerful Trello integrations and how they can transform your workflow.

Key Trello Integrations and How to Use Them

1. Google Drive: Attach and Access Files Easily

Google Drive is one of the most widely used cloud storage solutions, and integrating it with Trello helps teams manage files efficiently.

Benefits of Trello + Google Drive Integration

- Attach Google Drive documents, spreadsheets, presentations, and PDFs directly to Trello cards.

- Preview files without leaving Trello.

- Automatically sync updated files, ensuring teams always access the latest versions.

- Use the Google Drive Power-Up to search for Drive files within Trello.

How to Set Up Google Drive Integration

1. Open your Trello board and click on **Power-Ups**.

2. Search for **Google Drive** and click **Enable**.

3. Open a Trello card, click **Attach File**, and choose **Google Drive**.

4. Select a file to attach – it will now stay linked to the card.

Pro Tip: You can create new Google Docs, Sheets, or Slides directly from a Trello card, keeping your work streamlined.

2. Slack: Improve Team Communication

Slack is one of the most popular team messaging tools, and integrating it with Trello makes collaboration smoother.

Benefits of Trello + Slack Integration

- Convert Slack messages into **Trello cards** instantly.

- Get **Trello notifications** in Slack when tasks are updated.

- Assign and update **Trello cards from Slack**, without switching apps.

- Improve **team communication** by linking Trello boards to Slack channels.

How to Set Up Slack Integration

1. In Trello, go to **Power-Ups** and search for **Slack**.

2. Click **Enable** and authorize Trello to connect with Slack.

3. Select a Slack channel where you want Trello updates to appear.

4. Use the **/trello** command in Slack to create and manage Trello tasks.

Pro Tip: Automate Slack notifications for due date reminders and task assignments to keep teams aligned.

3. Jira: Manage Software Development Projects

Jira is a leading tool for software development teams, and integrating it with Trello allows for seamless coordination between high-level planning and technical execution.

Benefits of Trello + Jira Integration

- Link Trello cards to Jira issues for better task tracking.

- Sync updates between Trello and Jira automatically.

- View Jira issue details directly in Trello without switching apps.

- Improve communication between development and business teams.

How to Set Up Jira Integration

1. In Trello, go to **Power-Ups** and search for **Jira**.

2. Click **Enable** and log into your **Jira account**.

3. Open a Trello card and click **Attach Issue** to link Jira tasks.

💡 **Pro Tip:** If your team uses Agile workflows, use Jira to manage sprints while keeping high-level planning in Trello.

---

4. Zapier: Automate Trello Workflows

Zapier is a powerful automation tool that connects Trello with over 2,000+ other apps, allowing for custom workflows.

Benefits of Trello + Zapier Integration

- Automate task creation in Trello when emails arrive in Gmail or Outlook.

- Sync Trello cards with Google Calendar to track due dates.

- Automatically add new Trello cards from form submissions (e.g., Google Forms, Typeform).

- Send automatic updates to Slack, email, or other apps.

How to Set Up Zapier Integration

1. Sign up for a Zapier account and select Trello as a connected app.

2. Choose an app (e.g., Gmail) and select a trigger (e.g., "When an email arrives with a specific subject").

3. Set an action (e.g., "Create a Trello card in a specific board").

4. Save the Zap and activate the automation.

💡 **Pro Tip:** Use Zapier to automatically assign team members to new Trello cards based on predefined rules.

5. Confluence: Enhance Documentation and Knowledge Sharing

Confluence is a knowledge management tool used by many teams for internal documentation.

Benefits of Trello + Confluence Integration

- Link Trello cards to Confluence pages for detailed documentation.

- Create meeting notes in Confluence and link them to Trello boards.

- Embed Trello boards inside Confluence to track project progress.

How to Set Up Confluence Integration

1. In Trello, go to Power-Ups and search for Confluence.

2. Click Enable and log into your Confluence account.

3. Open a Trello card and attach a Confluence page for quick reference.

💡 **Pro Tip:** Use Confluence for detailed project documentation while keeping action items in Trello.

Final Thoughts: Supercharging Trello with Integrations

Integrating Trello with other essential tools transforms it into a powerful, all-in-one productivity hub. Whether you're managing projects, automating tasks, or improving team communication, these integrations provide seamless efficiency.

✅ **Google Drive** – Attach and manage files effortlessly.
✅ **Slack** – Improve real-time team collaboration.
✅ **Jira** – Sync development tasks with project planning.
✅ **Zapier** – Automate workflows across multiple apps.
✅ **Confluence** – Enhance documentation and knowledge sharing.

By leveraging these Power-Ups, you can reduce manual work, increase efficiency, and enhance productivity across your team. Now that you understand Trello's advanced capabilities, you're ready to explore best practices for organizing Trello boards efficiently in the next chapter! 🚀

CHAPTER VI
Advanced Trello Tips and Best Practices

6.1 Organizing Your Boards for Maximum Efficiency

6.1.1 Structuring Boards for Personal Use

Trello is a highly versatile tool that can be tailored to suit personal organization needs. Whether you're managing daily tasks, planning long-term goals, or tracking personal projects, structuring your Trello boards effectively will significantly enhance your productivity.

In this section, we'll explore how to structure Trello boards for personal use, including best practices, real-life examples, and customization tips to make Trello work best for you.

Why Use Trello for Personal Organization?

Many people associate Trello with team collaboration and business project management, but it is equally powerful for personal productivity. Here's why Trello is a great personal organization tool:

✓ Visual Task Management – Trello's Kanban-style boards make it easy to see everything at a glance.
✓ Flexibility – You can structure boards exactly how you want.
✓ Cross-Platform Access – Manage tasks on your desktop, tablet, or phone anytime.
✓ Automation and Integrations – Use Butler and Power-Ups to automate tasks and sync

with other apps.

☑ Free to Use – The free plan is more than enough for most personal users.

Now, let's dive into how you can structure Trello for personal use effectively.

Step 1: Choosing the Right Board Structure

The first step in organizing your personal Trello boards is choosing a structure that fits your needs. Here are a few common ways people use Trello for personal organization:

1. Daily Task and To-Do List Board

A simple daily planner board is great for tracking tasks, prioritizing work, and maintaining productivity.

📌 Recommended List Structure:

- Inbox – Brain dump tasks as they come to mind.

- Today – Move tasks you want to complete today.

- In Progress – Tasks you're actively working on.

- Completed – Move finished tasks here.

- Backlog/Future Tasks – Store long-term ideas or non-urgent tasks.

This setup helps you stay focused on daily priorities while keeping track of future tasks.

2. Personal Goals and Habit Tracking Board

If you're working on self-improvement, fitness, learning new skills, or other personal goals, Trello can help track progress.

📌 Recommended List Structure:

- Goals for the Year – List your major objectives.

- Monthly Goals – Break down yearly goals into manageable chunks.

- Weekly Goals – Specific tasks to achieve monthly objectives.

- Daily Habits – Track habits like exercise, reading, or meditation.

- Completed Achievements – Celebrate milestones and successes!

You can use labels (e.g., health, finance, personal development) to categorize different goals.

3. Project Management for Personal Side Projects

If you're working on personal projects (blogging, writing a book, coding, home renovations, etc.), Trello is an excellent way to track progress.

📌 Recommended List Structure:

- Ideas/Brainstorming – Capture all your project ideas.

- Planning – Outline project goals, timelines, and resources.

- In Progress – Tasks currently being worked on.

- Testing/Review – Tasks that need evaluation or feedback.

- Completed – Finished work!

For complex projects, you can add checklists inside cards to break tasks into smaller steps.

4. Meal Planning and Grocery Shopping Board

Meal planning is an excellent way to save time, eat healthier, and reduce food waste. Trello makes meal planning fun and easy!

📌 Recommended List Structure:

- Recipe Ideas – Store your favorite meals.

- This Week's Meals – Plan meals for the week.

- Grocery List – Add ingredients you need to buy.

- Meal Prep Tasks – Track what needs to be prepped ahead.

Power-ups like Google Drive (for storing recipes) or Calendar (to schedule meals) can make meal planning even more efficient.

Step 2: Optimizing Board Layout for Efficiency

Once you've chosen the right structure, follow these best practices to keep your Trello board organized and effective.

Use Labels for Categorization

Labels help organize tasks visually. For example:
☞ **Priority Levels:** High (●), Medium (☐), Low (☐)
🏠 **Categories:** Work, Home, Finance, Health, Hobbies
🗓 **Time-Based:** Urgent, This Week, This Month, Future

Set Due Dates and Reminders

- Assign due dates to important tasks so Trello reminds you when they're due.

- Use Butler automation to move overdue tasks to a "Urgent" list.

Use Checklists for Subtasks

Instead of cluttering your board with too many cards, add checklists inside cards.
For example, a "Grocery Shopping" card could have:
✓ Milk
✓ Eggs
✓ Vegetables

Archive or Delete Old Cards

Regularly clean up your board by archiving completed tasks or deleting unnecessary items.

Create a "Done" List Instead of Deleting Tasks

Instead of deleting finished tasks, move them to a "Completed" list. This helps track progress over time.

Utilize Card Attachments

Attach important files, images, or links to Trello cards so everything is stored in one place.

Step 3: Enhancing Your Board with Power-Ups and Automation

Power-ups and automation features can take your board to the next level.

Best Power-Ups for Personal Boards

🗓 Calendar View – See tasks with due dates in a calendar format.
☐ Recurring Tasks – Automate repeated tasks like bill payments or weekly goals.

⬇ Google Drive – Store and access documents directly from Trello.

💇 Custom Fields – Add extra details to cards, like priority levels or estimated time.

Using Butler for Personal Task Automation

Trello's Butler automation can help streamline your workflow:

- Automatically move cards from "Today" to "In Progress" when you start a task.

- Set recurring tasks (e.g., "Pay rent" every month).

- Create automatic reminders for overdue tasks.

Step 4: Maintaining Your Board for Long-Term Productivity

Setting up your board is just the first step—keeping it updated is key! Follow these simple habits:

✅ Review your board daily – Spend 5 minutes checking and updating tasks.

✅ Do a weekly cleanup – Move completed tasks, archive old cards, and plan the week ahead.

✅ Adjust your board as needed – Customize lists and labels to fit your changing workflow.

Final Thoughts: Make Trello Work for You!

Trello is an incredibly flexible tool that can be customized to fit any personal productivity system. Whether you're using it for daily to-do lists, personal goal tracking, side projects, or even meal planning, the key is to structure your board in a way that works for you.

By choosing the right structure, optimizing your board layout, using Power-Ups, and maintaining consistency, you can maximize your efficiency and stay organized effortlessly.

✏ Now that you've learned how to organize Trello for personal use, in the next section, we'll explore how to set up Trello for business and team collaboration!

6.1.2 Best Practices for Business and Team Boards

Trello is widely used in business environments to streamline workflows, enhance collaboration, and improve overall efficiency. However, without proper organization, team boards can become cluttered and chaotic, reducing their effectiveness. This section explores best practices for structuring business and team boards to maximize efficiency and maintain smooth operations.

1. Establish a Clear Board Structure

For businesses, Trello boards should be designed with a clear purpose and workflow. A well-structured board improves productivity and prevents confusion.

Define the Purpose of Each Board

- Avoid using one massive board for everything—create separate boards for different departments or projects.

- Examples of effective business boards include:

    - Project Management Board – Tracks projects from initiation to completion.

    - Sales and CRM Board – Manages leads, prospects, and customer interactions.

    - Marketing Campaign Board – Organizes marketing tasks, content calendars, and advertising strategies.

    - HR and Onboarding Board – Helps manage recruitment, training, and employee onboarding.

- Use board descriptions to clarify the board's purpose for all team members.

Set Up Consistent List Structures

- Use standardized list names across similar boards to make navigation easier.

- Common list structures include:

    - To Do → In Progress → Review → Completed (Task Progress)

    - Ideas → Planned → Executing → Evaluating (Strategic Planning)

- o Backlog → Sprint → Testing → Released (Agile & Scrum Workflows)
- o New Leads → Contacted → Proposal Sent → Negotiation → Closed Deal (Sales Pipeline)
- Limit the number of lists to avoid overwhelming team members.

2. Optimize Cards for Effective Communication

Trello's cards represent individual tasks or pieces of work. Properly managing them ensures smooth collaboration within a team.

Use Clear and Descriptive Card Titles

- Instead of vague titles like *"Meeting"*, use "Marketing Team Meeting - Q2 Strategy Discussion (April 5, 2025)".
- Include task owner names in titles if necessary: *"[John] Draft Q3 Marketing Report"*.

Assign Responsibilities and Due Dates

- Every card should have a designated owner to prevent confusion.
- Use due dates and enable calendar view to track deadlines.
- Set reminders so team members receive notifications before deadlines.

Leverage Checklists for Subtasks

- Break down complex tasks into checklists to improve clarity.
- Example checklist for a product launch card:
    - o ☐ Finalize product design
    - o ☐ Create marketing materials
    - o ☐ Plan launch event
    - o ☐ Publish website updates
    - o ☐ Send press release

Utilize Labels for Categorization

- **Color-coded labels** make it easy to categorize tasks:

  - ⬤ High Priority

  - ☐ Low Priority

  - ⬤ Urgent

  - ☐ Pending Approval

- Standardize label meanings across all team boards.

3. Maintain an Efficient Workflow

To keep business and team boards productive, it's important to implement workflow management strategies.

Implement WIP (Work in Progress) Limits

- Avoid overloading team members by setting Work in Progress (WIP) limits.

- Example: Limit "In Progress" list to a maximum of 5 cards per person.

- Helps teams focus on finishing tasks before starting new ones.

Use Automation to Reduce Manual Work

- Enable Butler automation to move cards, set due dates, or assign tasks based on conditions.

- Automate recurring tasks (e.g., "Weekly Team Meeting Agenda" card created every Monday).

Regularly Review and Archive Completed Tasks

- Move finished tasks to an "Archive" or "Completed" list to keep boards clutter-free.

- Schedule weekly cleanups to remove old or irrelevant tasks.

4. Enhance Team Collaboration and Transparency

Trello should serve as a central hub for team communication to improve transparency and accountability.

Use the Comments Section for Discussions

- Encourage team members to comment on cards instead of using emails.

- Mention teammates using "@username" for quick notifications.

- Use comments for status updates, such as:

    o "Task 50% complete – waiting for approval from manager."

    o "Blocked by missing client feedback – rescheduling for next week."

Set Up a Clear Communication Protocol

- Establish guidelines on when to use Trello vs. email vs. meetings.

- Define response times for task updates (e.g., all comments should be addressed within 24 hours).

Utilize Team Members' Permissions Wisely

- **Admins**: Control board settings and manage users.

- **Normal Members**: Can add/edit cards but not delete boards.

- **Observers**: Read-only access for external stakeholders.

---

5. Integrate Trello with Business Tools

To improve efficiency, integrate Trello with tools commonly used in business environments.

Connect Trello with Project Management Tools

- **Jira** (For software development teams).

- **Asana** (For task synchronization across teams).

Sync Trello with Communication Platforms

- **Slack**: Get Trello updates directly in Slack channels.

- **Microsoft Teams**: Access Trello boards within MS Teams.

Automate Workflow with Power-Ups

- **Google Drive**: Attach documents to Trello cards.

- **Zapier**: Automate workflows between Trello and other apps.

- **Time Tracking**: Use Power-Ups like **Clockify** to monitor task durations.

6. Monitor and Improve Board Performance

For a business to continuously improve, it's important to track Trello board performance and refine workflows accordingly.

Conduct Weekly or Monthly Board Reviews

- Identify bottlenecks in workflows.

- Assess task completion rates to improve productivity.

- Check if WIP limits and automation are effective.

Track Key Performance Metrics

- Average Task Completion Time – Are tasks being completed on time?

- Number of Overdue Tasks – How often are deadlines missed?

- Task Distribution Among Team Members – Is the workload balanced?

Adjust and Optimize Board Layouts

- Remove unnecessary lists that slow down workflow.

- Update naming conventions for better clarity.

- Consolidate duplicate tasks to avoid confusion.

Final Thoughts

Organizing Trello boards for business and team use requires strategic planning and disciplined execution. By implementing best practices such as structured workflows, effective communication, automation, and integration with other tools, teams can enhance productivity and collaboration.

With these optimizations, your Trello boards will transform into powerful business management tools, helping your team stay on top of tasks, streamline processes, and achieve goals efficiently.

Next, we'll explore how Trello can be adapted for different use cases such as Project Management, Personal Productivity, and Agile Workflows. 🚀

6.2 Trello for Different Use Cases

6.2.1 Trello for Project Management

Trello is an excellent tool for project management due to its flexibility, visual organization, and ease of collaboration. Whether you are managing a small personal project or coordinating a complex team effort, Trello's Kanban-based system provides a clear, structured way to track progress.

This section explores how Trello can be effectively used for project management, covering how to set up a project board, organize tasks, collaborate with teams, use automation, and integrate with other tools to improve efficiency.

Why Use Trello for Project Management?

Trello provides a **clear and visual approach** to managing projects, making it easier to track progress and ensure nothing is overlooked. Some key benefits of using Trello for project management include:

- **Simplicity** – Trello's user-friendly design allows teams to get started quickly.

- **Flexibility** – Adapt Trello to different project workflows, including Agile, Scrum, or traditional methods.

- **Collaboration** – Assign tasks, set deadlines, and communicate with team members within Trello.

- **Automation** – Reduce manual work with Trello's Butler automation and integrations.

- **Transparency** – Everyone involved in the project can see the progress in real-time.

By setting up a well-structured board and following best practices, Trello can help teams increase productivity and ensure successful project completion.

Setting Up a Trello Board for Project Management

1. Creating a Project Board

The first step in managing a project with Trello is creating a dedicated board for your project.

◆ Go to Trello → Click "Create new board" → Name it according to your project (e.g., "Marketing Campaign 2025" or "Product Launch Plan").
◆ Choose a background to make it visually distinct.
◆ Set board visibility (Private, Team, or Public) based on project needs.

2. Structuring Lists for a Project Workflow

Trello's lists represent different stages of a project. Common structures include:

✅ Basic Workflow (To-Do, In Progress, Done)

- **To-Do**: All planned tasks that need to be completed.

- **In Progress**: Tasks currently being worked on.

- **Done**: Completed tasks.

☐ Advanced Project Workflow

For larger teams and complex projects, you can use:

- **Backlog**: Future tasks or ideas not yet started.

- **Sprint Planning**: Tasks scheduled for an upcoming sprint (for Agile teams).

- **In Progress**: Active tasks.

- **Review/Approval**: Tasks waiting for review or approval.

- **Completed**: Finalized and delivered tasks.

This setup provides clear visibility into task progression.

Organizing Project Tasks with Trello Cards

Each task in a project is represented as a Trello card, which can be customized with details such as:

- Title & Description → Clearly define the task's purpose.
- Checklists → Break down larger tasks into smaller subtasks.
- Due Dates → Assign deadlines to keep tasks on track.
- Labels & Tags → Categorize tasks by priority, department, or project phase.
- Attachments → Upload files, documents, or links relevant to the task.
- Comments & Mentions → Enable discussions and feedback within the task.

💡 *Tip:* Keep card titles short but descriptive (e.g., "Finalize Product Design Mockups" instead of just "Design Task").

Enhancing Team Collaboration in Trello

One of Trello's strengths is its ability to enhance team collaboration by ensuring everyone stays informed and aligned.

1. Assigning Tasks to Team Members

- Click on a Trello card → Add team members who are responsible for the task.
- Members receive notifications when assigned.
- Assign multiple members for collaborative tasks.

2. Communicating Within Trello

- Use the comments section in each card to ask questions, provide updates, or tag teammates.
- Tag members using @mentions (e.g., "@John Please review this document").
- Use emojis 👍✅🔥 to highlight important points.

3. Setting Up Notifications

- Team members receive real-time updates when a task is updated.
- Use the "Watch" feature to follow specific cards or boards.

💡 *Best Practice:* Keep all discussions within Trello cards instead of using external emails or chat tools.

Using Trello Automation for Project Management

Trello's Butler automation helps streamline repetitive project management tasks.

1. Automating Task Assignments

Example: Automatically assign a "Design" task to the design team.

- Click Automation (Butler) → Rules → Create a Rule.
- Set Trigger (e.g., "When a new card is added to 'To-Do'").
- Add Action (e.g., "Assign to @DesignerTeam").

2. Automating Task Progression

Example: Automatically move a card to "In Progress" when a checklist is 50% completed.

- Click Automation (Butler) → Rules → Create a Rule.
- Set Trigger (e.g., "When checklist items are completed").
- Set Action (e.g., "Move card to 'In Progress'").

💡 *Tip:* Use automation for reminders, due date alerts, and repetitive tasks to save time.

Integrating Trello with Other Project Management Tools

To enhance productivity, Trello integrates with **various external tools**:

- **Google Drive & Dropbox** → Attach project documents directly to Trello cards.
- **Slack & Microsoft Teams** → Receive Trello updates in team communication channels.
- **Jira & GitHub** → Sync development tasks between engineering and management teams.
- **Evernote & Confluence** → Link notes and project documentation.

💡 *Best Practice:* Use Trello Power-Ups to activate these integrations without leaving Trello.

Tracking Project Progress and Performance in Trello

Trello provides various ways to monitor progress:

1. Trello Board Views

- **Calendar View** → Track tasks with deadlines.

- **Timeline View** → Visualize project phases.

- **Dashboard View** → Get an overview of project metrics.

2. Using Trello Reports & Analytics

- **Butler Reports** → Generate summaries of completed tasks.

- **External Tools (Trello Power-Ups)** → Connect Trello with reporting tools like **Google Sheets**.

💡 *Tip:* Conduct weekly project reviews using Trello's reporting features.

Best Practices for Using Trello in Project Management

✅ Standardize naming conventions (e.g., "[Marketing] Social Media Campaign Q2").
✅ Use labels for task categorization (e.g., High Priority 🔥, Client Task 💼).
✅ Schedule regular board check-ins (e.g., Weekly team stand-ups).
✅ Archive old cards and lists to keep boards clean.
✅ Keep boards visually organized with a clear structure.

Conclusion

Trello is a powerful, flexible, and user-friendly tool for managing projects of any size. By setting up a well-structured board, assigning tasks efficiently, leveraging automation, and integrating with other tools, teams can achieve better organization, collaboration, and productivity.

Now that you understand how to use Trello for project management, let's explore how Trello can be applied to personal productivity in the next section! 🚀

6.2.2 Trello for Personal Productivity

Trello is widely known for its use in team collaboration and project management, but it is also a powerful personal productivity tool. Whether you need to manage your daily to-do lists, organize personal projects, track habits, or plan long-term goals, Trello provides a visual, flexible, and structured way to stay on top of everything.

This section will explore how you can leverage Trello for personal productivity, including how to set up personal boards, create effective workflows, use automation, and integrate Trello with other tools.

Why Use Trello for Personal Productivity?

Before diving into the details, let's understand why Trello is an excellent choice for personal task management:

✓ **Visual Organization** – The Kanban-style interface makes it easy to see what needs to be done at a glance.

✓ **Flexibility** – You can customize boards, lists, and cards to fit your workflow.

✓ **Task Prioritization** – Labels, due dates, and checklists help you prioritize tasks efficiently.

✓ **Accessibility** – Trello syncs across devices, ensuring that you have your tasks wherever you go.

✓ **Automation** – Features like Butler automation help reduce repetitive work.

✓ **Integration** – You can connect Trello with Google Calendar, Evernote, and other productivity tools.

Now, let's explore how to set up Trello for personal use in different productivity scenarios.

Setting Up a Personal Productivity System in Trello

The first step to using Trello effectively for personal productivity is to create a structured and efficient system. Below is a step-by-step guide to setting up your personal Trello board.

1. Creating Your Personal Productivity Board

To start, create a new Trello board and give it a name that suits your needs, such as:

- "Personal Productivity"
- "Daily Planner"
- "My Life Dashboard"

You can then customize the background and board settings to make it visually appealing.

---

2. Structuring Your Lists for Productivity

The key to using Trello effectively is setting up lists that match your workflow. Here are some common list structures you can use:

Method 1: Simple To-Do List

If you prefer a basic setup, use **three core lists**:
📝 **To-Do** – Tasks you need to complete.
🚀 **In Progress** – Tasks you are currently working on.
✅ **Completed** – Tasks you have finished.

Method 2: Daily & Weekly Organization

For better time management, use:
📅 **Today** – Tasks for the current day.
📆 **This Week** – Important tasks for the week.
☐ **Upcoming** – Future tasks that you need to plan ahead.
🏆 **Done** – Completed tasks (can be archived periodically).

Method 3: The Eisenhower Matrix for Prioritization

Use Trello to apply the **Eisenhower Matrix** to prioritize tasks:

🔥 **Urgent & Important** – Must be done immediately.

☐ **Important but Not Urgent** – Schedule these tasks.

⚠☐ **Urgent but Not Important** – Delegate or minimize.

☐ **Neither Urgent Nor Important** – Consider eliminating.

Using Cards Effectively for Personal Tasks

Once your lists are set up, create **cards** for individual tasks and customize them for better productivity.

1. Adding Essential Task Details

Each **Trello card** represents a **task** or **activity**. When adding a new task, include:

✅ **A clear task title** – Keep it short and descriptive.

📝 **A detailed description** – Include important details, subtasks, or links.

📅 **Due dates** – Set deadlines to stay on track.

🏷 **Labels** – Categorize tasks by urgency, project, or type.

📎 **Attachments** – Add documents, images, or links for reference.

✅ **Checklists** – Break tasks into smaller steps for better tracking.

2. Using Labels and Tags for Prioritization

Trello allows you to **color-code** tasks with **labels**. Some useful labels include:

🔴 **High Priority** – Must be done ASAP.

☐ **Medium Priority** – Important but not urgent.

☐ **Low Priority** – Can be done later.

⬤ **Personal Projects** – Tasks related to hobbies, learning, or side projects.

Automating Personal Tasks with Trello Butler

To reduce manual work, use Trello's Butler automation to streamline your workflow.

1. Creating Automation Rules

Examples of useful Butler automation:

✓ Automatically move completed tasks to the "Done" list.
✓ Set recurring tasks (e.g., "Weekly review" every Sunday).
✓ Add due dates automatically when a card is moved to a specific list.

2. Using Scheduled Commands

You can schedule automatic reminders and recurring tasks. For example:

- Every Monday at 9 AM, create a new "Weekly Goals" card in your board.

- Every day at 7 AM, move overdue tasks to the "Today" list.

Integrating Trello with Other Productivity Tools

Trello works even better when combined with **other productivity tools**.

◆ **Google Calendar** – Sync Trello tasks with your calendar for better scheduling.
◆ **Evernote** – Link Trello with Evernote to manage notes and ideas.
◆ **Google Drive & Dropbox** – Attach files directly to Trello cards.
◆ **Pomodone** – Use Trello with the Pomodoro Technique to improve focus.

These integrations ensure a seamless workflow and better time management.

Examples of Using Trello for Personal Productivity

1. Daily Task Management

Use Trello to create a morning routine and track daily habits.

- Morning Routine List: Exercise, meditation, reading, breakfast.

- Work Tasks List: Emails, meetings, deadlines.

- Personal Projects List: Learning, hobbies, home tasks.

2. Goal Tracking

Set up a board for **personal goals**:

📌 **List 1: Yearly Goals** – Major objectives for the year.
📌 **List 2: Monthly Milestones** – Break yearly goals into monthly tasks.
📌 **List 3: Weekly Progress** – Track weekly achievements.

3. Budget and Expense Tracking

Create a board to manage monthly expenses and savings goals.

💰 **List 1: Income Sources**
💳 **List 2: Fixed Expenses** (Rent, subscriptions, bills)
☐ **List 3: Variable Expenses** (Shopping, dining, travel)
📊 **List 4: Savings & Investments**

Final Thoughts

Trello is a powerful and flexible tool that can dramatically boost your personal productivity. By setting up structured boards, using labels, automation, and integrations, you can create an efficient system that keeps you organized and on track.

✅ Create lists that fit your workflow.
✅ Use cards effectively with labels, checklists, and due dates.
✅ Automate tasks with Butler to save time.
✅ Integrate Trello with other tools for a seamless experience.

By following these best practices, you can transform Trello into your ultimate personal productivity hub! 🚀

6.2.3 Trello for Agile Workflows

Agile methodologies have become increasingly popular in modern project management, especially in software development, marketing, and product management. Agile focuses on flexibility, collaboration, and iterative progress, allowing teams to adapt quickly to changes. Trello, with its visual and intuitive Kanban-style interface, is an excellent tool for managing Agile workflows effectively.

In this section, we will explore how Trello can be adapted to support Agile methodologies, including Scrum and Kanban workflows, sprint planning, backlog management, and team collaboration. Whether you're a Scrum Master, Product Owner, or team member, this guide will help you leverage Trello to streamline your Agile process.

What is Agile?

Agile is a project management philosophy that emphasizes:
✓ Iterative development – Delivering small, functional increments instead of a full product at once.
✓ Continuous feedback – Regular check-ins and refinements based on user and stakeholder input.
✓ Collaboration – Encouraging communication within teams and across departments.
✓ Flexibility – Adapting to changes rather than rigidly following a pre-defined plan.

Trello provides the perfect digital workspace for implementing Agile, making it easy for teams to visualize their workflow, prioritize tasks, and track progress.

Setting Up an Agile Trello Board

A well-structured Trello board is essential for efficient Agile execution. Here's how to set up a board tailored for Agile workflows:

Step 1: Creating an Agile Board

1. Open Trello and create a new board.

2. Choose a clear and descriptive name (e.g., "Sprint Board - Team Alpha").

3. Select an appropriate background for visual clarity.

Step 2: Defining Your Lists

A Trello board in Agile typically includes the following lists:

- Backlog – A collection of tasks, ideas, and user stories that need to be worked on.

- To-Do (Sprint Backlog) – Tasks planned for the current sprint.

- In Progress – Tasks currently being worked on by team members.

- Code Review / Testing – Tasks that need validation before being marked as complete.

- Done – Completed tasks that meet the acceptance criteria.

These lists help teams visualize the workflow, track tasks, and maintain clarity on project status.

Using Trello for Scrum Workflows

Scrum is a popular Agile framework that divides work into sprints (time-boxed iterations of 1-4 weeks). Trello can effectively support Scrum processes with the following features:

Sprint Planning with Trello

- At the beginning of each sprint, move selected tasks from Backlog to To-Do (Sprint Backlog).

- Assign team members to each task using Trello's "Members" feature.

- Use checklists within cards to break down complex tasks into subtasks.

- Set due dates to ensure tasks are completed within the sprint duration.

Tracking Sprint Progress

- Move cards across lists (e.g., from "In Progress" to "Code Review") as work progresses.

- Add labels to highlight priorities (e.g., High Priority, Bug Fix, Feature).

- Use Power-Ups like "Sprint Burndown Charts" to track overall progress.

Daily Standups with Trello

- Use Trello as a visual aid during daily standups to review task statuses.

- Team members update their assigned cards with comments like:

    - ✅ What was completed yesterday?

    - ☐ What is being worked on today?

    - 🚧 What blockers or challenges exist?

Implementing Kanban with Trello

Kanban is another Agile approach that focuses on continuous delivery and workflow efficiency. Trello's Kanban-style board is perfect for implementing this methodology.

Key Kanban Principles in Trello

1. Visualize work – Trello's card-based system makes workflows transparent and easy to understand.

2. Limit Work in Progress (WIP) – Use Trello to enforce WIP limits, ensuring team members don't take on too many tasks at once.

3. Measure cycle time – Use Trello's Card Aging Power-Up to track how long tasks remain in each stage.

Using Trello for Continuous Delivery

- New work items go into the Backlog.

- Each task moves through To-Do → In Progress → Testing → Deployment.

- Completed tasks move to Done, keeping the workflow fluid and efficient.

Managing Product Backlogs in Trello

A product backlog is a dynamic list of features, bug fixes, and improvements that must be addressed in future iterations. Trello makes backlog management simple:

- Create a dedicated "Backlog" list to store all ideas, requests, and feature improvements.

- Use labels to categorize backlog items (e.g., Feature Request, Bug, Improvement).

- Prioritize tasks by dragging and dropping them within the list based on urgency.

- Archive old or irrelevant cards to keep the backlog clean.

💡 *Tip: Use the "Voting" Power-Up to let stakeholders prioritize feature requests!*

Enhancing Agile Workflows with Trello Power-Ups

Trello offers **Power-Ups** (integrations) that enhance Agile capabilities:

✅ **Calendar Power-Up** – Helps track sprint deadlines.
✅ **Scrum for Trello** – Adds Agile-specific features like story points.
✅ **Burndown Charts** – Visualize sprint progress with Power-Ups like "Agile Reports".
✅ **Slack Integration** – Receive Trello updates in Slack for instant communication.

Using these **Power-Ups**, Agile teams can **optimize** their workflow and boost productivity.

Automating Agile Processes with Butler

Trello's Butler Automation tool helps reduce manual workload and streamline Agile processes.

Examples of Butler Automation for Agile Teams:

- Automatically move cards to "Done" when checklists are completed.

- Send reminders to team members when tasks approach their due dates.

- Assign tasks automatically when a new card is added to a sprint backlog.

This automation ensures that Agile teams can focus on high-impact work instead of repetitive administrative tasks.

Common Challenges and Best Practices

While Trello is powerful for Agile, teams may encounter challenges. Here's how to overcome them:

❌ Overloaded boards → Regularly clean up old tasks and archive completed cards.
❌ Lack of sprint planning → Use checklists and labels to maintain structured sprints.
❌ Unclear responsibilities → Assign owners to every card for accountability.
❌ Too many work-in-progress tasks → Set WIP limits to prevent burnout.

✅ Best Practice: Hold regular retrospectives to review what worked well and what needs improvement!

Conclusion: Why Use Trello for Agile?

Trello provides an intuitive, flexible, and powerful platform for managing Agile workflows, whether you're following Scrum, Kanban, or a hybrid approach.

⭐ Easy setup and customization for Agile teams.
⭐ Real-time collaboration and transparency.
⭐ Integrations with Agile tools like Jira, Slack, and Google Drive.
⭐ Automation to minimize repetitive tasks.

By following these strategies, teams can effectively manage Agile projects and maximize productivity using Trello.

6.3 Troubleshooting Common Issues

6.3.1 Handling Board and Card Overload

As you continue using Trello, you may find that your boards become cluttered with too many cards, lists, and activities. This can make it harder to manage tasks effectively and reduce the overall productivity benefits that Trello offers. In this section, we will explore strategies to prevent and resolve board and card overload, ensuring that your Trello workspace remains organized, efficient, and easy to navigate.

Understanding Board and Card Overload

Board and card overload occurs when:

- A Trello board contains too many lists and becomes difficult to navigate.

- Individual lists have an excessive number of cards, making it hard to track progress.

- Too many incomplete tasks pile up, leading to reduced productivity.

- Users struggle to find relevant information due to clutter and lack of organization.

- Notifications become overwhelming, making it hard to focus on priorities.

These issues often arise in growing teams, fast-paced projects, or when Trello is used without a structured workflow. The key to managing overload is simplification, prioritization, and automation.

1. Structuring Your Boards for Clarity

Limiting the Number of Lists on a Board

A well-structured Trello board should have a clear, concise workflow with an optimal number of lists. Consider these approaches:

- Follow the Kanban model: Use the standard *To-Do → In Progress → Done* structure.

- Categorize tasks by priority: Create lists like *High Priority, Medium Priority, Low Priority*.

- Group tasks by timeframes: Use lists such as *This Week, Next Week, Future Tasks*.

- Keep active tasks visible: Archive or move completed tasks to prevent overcrowding.

◆ **Tip:** If your board has too many lists, consider creating multiple **linked boards** instead.

Using Sub-Boards for Large Projects

Instead of having one massive board for everything, break projects into **sub-boards**:

- Main Project Board: An overview with high-level tasks.

- Task-Specific Boards: Separate boards for areas like Marketing, Development, or Sales.

- Team-Specific Boards: A dedicated board for each team or department.

◆ **Tip:** Use Trello's Workspace feature to group related boards together for easy navigation.

2. Managing Card Overload Effectively

Setting Limits on Active Cards

One of the best ways to manage card overload is by enforcing Work In Progress (WIP) limits:

- Limit the number of tasks in the *In Progress* list to prevent multitasking overload.

- Use labels to categorize urgent vs. non-urgent tasks.

- Archive completed cards regularly to reduce visual clutter.

◆ **Tip:** Use Butler automation to send reminders when too many cards are active in a list.

Using Checklists to Avoid Overcrowding

Instead of creating a new card for every minor task, use checklists within cards:

- Break down a large task into subtasks using checklists.

- Assign checklist items to specific team members.

- Convert a checklist item into a separate card when needed.

◆ **Tip:** Use Butler rules to automatically move completed checklist items to a "Done" list.

3. Automating Task Management to Reduce Overload

Setting Up Automated Workflows with Butler

Trello's Butler automation can help manage board overload by:

- Automatically moving completed cards to an archive list.

- Sending reminders for overdue tasks.

- Assigning tasks based on triggers, such as due dates or labels.

◆ **Tip:** Set up a rule that moves old cards to an "Archive" list once they haven't been updated in 30 days.

Using Power-Ups for Better Organization

Power-Ups can enhance task management and prevent overload:

- Calendar Power-Up: Visualize due dates in a calendar view.

- Card Aging Power-Up: Fade out inactive cards to highlight priority tasks.

- Custom Fields Power-Up: Add additional information to cards without overcrowding them.

◆ **Tip:** Limit the number of Power-Ups to prevent unnecessary complexity.

4. Keeping Notifications Under Control

Managing Notification Overload

If you receive too many Trello notifications, consider:

- Unsubscribing from irrelevant cards to avoid unnecessary alerts.

- Using Trello's notification settings to get updates only on essential changes.

- Setting up Slack or email integrations for consolidated notifications.

◆ **Tip:** Enable Trello's "Daily Summary" email to receive one digest of updates instead of multiple alerts.

5. Regular Maintenance and Clean-Up

Archiving and Deleting Old Cards

To keep your board clutter-free:

- Archive cards that are no longer needed instead of keeping them visible.

- Delete old and irrelevant boards that are no longer in use.

- Review boards regularly to remove outdated information.

◆ **Tip:** Set a quarterly board review to clean up unnecessary data.

Conducting Periodic Board Audits

Assign a board manager who:

- Regularly checks for duplicate or outdated tasks.

- Ensures the board layout remains simple and efficient.

- Removes inactive members and reorganizes workflows when necessary.

◆ **Tip:** Schedule a monthly review session with your team to discuss board improvements.

Conclusion: Mastering Board and Card Overload

Trello is a powerful tool, but without proper organization and maintenance, it can become overwhelming. By structuring boards effectively, managing card overload, leveraging automation, and maintaining regular clean-ups, you can ensure that Trello remains a highly efficient and stress-free task management tool.

✅ Keep boards simple – Avoid excessive lists and use linked boards.
✅ Manage cards wisely – Use checklists, labels, and WIP limits.
✅ Automate tasks – Use Butler to move, assign, and remind users automatically.
✅ Control notifications – Customize settings to reduce distractions.
✅ Maintain regularly – Archive old cards and conduct board audits.

By following these best practices, you can prevent Trello overload and make your workflow more productive and manageable. 🎯

📌 **Next Step:** In the next section, we'll explore **how to troubleshoot notification and access problems**, ensuring smooth collaboration within Trello! 🚀

6.3.2 Fixing Notification and Access Problems

Trello is a powerful tool for task management and collaboration, but like any software, users may encounter issues—especially with notifications and access controls. If notifications aren't working as expected or users are having trouble accessing boards, it can disrupt workflows and cause miscommunication.

In this section, we will explore the most common notification and access-related issues in Trello and provide practical solutions to resolve them.

Understanding Trello's Notification System

Before troubleshooting, it's important to understand how Trello notifications work. Trello provides real-time updates through multiple notification channels:

- **In-app notifications**: Appear as a red badge in the Trello interface.
- **Email notifications**: Sent to your registered email address.

- **Push notifications**: Available on mobile devices.

- **Browser notifications**: Alerts on your desktop when using Trello in a web browser.

Trello notifications only trigger when a user is directly involved in an activity, such as:

✔ When you are **mentioned** in a comment (@username).

✔ When you are **added to a card, board, or checklist**.

✔ When someone **moves, archives, or deletes a card you are assigned to**.

✔ When a **due date is approaching** (if notifications are enabled).

If you're not receiving notifications, the issue may be related to settings, permissions, or external factors such as email filters.

Troubleshooting Notification Issues

1. Not Receiving Email Notifications

If you are not receiving Trello email notifications, follow these steps to resolve the issue:

Step 1: Check Your Email Notification Preferences

1. Click on your **profile picture** in Trello (top-right corner).

2. Go to **Settings > Notifications**.

3. Ensure that **email notifications** are **enabled**.

4. Check the notification frequency setting—Trello allows **Instant, Periodic, or Never** for email alerts.

Step 2: Check Spam or Promotions Folder

- Sometimes, Trello emails get **filtered as spam** or land in the **Promotions** tab (for Gmail users).

- Search for **"Trello"** in your email inbox to locate lost notifications.

- If you find a Trello email in spam, mark it as **"Not Spam"** to ensure future emails arrive in your inbox.

Step 3: Whitelist Trello's Email Address

- Add notifications@trello.com to your email contact list or whitelist it in your email settings.

- If you use **corporate email**, ask your **IT team** to allow emails from Trello.

Step 4: Ensure You Are Subscribed to Boards and Cards

- Trello only sends notifications if you are **watching** a board, list, or card.

- Open the board and click on **"Show Menu" > "More" > "Watch"** to receive notifications.

Step 5: Check for Email Delays

- Trello's **Periodic** email setting may delay notifications.

- Switch to **Instant** notifications for immediate updates.

2. Not Receiving Push Notifications on Mobile

If Trello push notifications are not working on **iOS** or **Android**, try the following:

Step 1: Enable Notifications in Trello App

1. Open the Trello mobile app.

2. Tap on your profile picture > Settings > Push Notifications.

3. Ensure that push notifications are turned on.

Step 2: Check Phone Notification Settings

- On iPhone:

  1. Go to **Settings > Notifications**.

  2. Find Trello and make sure **Allow Notifications** is enabled.

  3. Enable **Sounds, Badges, and Banners**.

- On Android:

1. Go to **Settings** > **Apps & Notifications**.

2. Locate **Trello** and tap on it.

3. Enable **Allow Notifications** and customize notification preferences.

Step 3: Log Out and Log Back In

- Sometimes, logging out of Trello and logging back in can **refresh push notifications**.

Step 4: Update the Trello App

- Ensure your Trello app is **up-to-date** to prevent notification issues caused by outdated versions.

Troubleshooting Access Issues

1. Cannot Access a Trello Board

If you are unable to access a Trello board, follow these steps:

Step 1: Check Your Internet Connection

- A weak or unstable internet connection can prevent Trello from loading properly.

- Try switching from Wi-Fi to mobile data (or vice versa) to see if the issue persists.

Step 2: Verify Your Permissions

- If you are not a member of a board, you cannot access it unless the board is public.

- Ask the board owner to invite you or check your access level.

Step 3: Confirm Board Visibility Settings

- If a board was changed from Public to Private, non-members will lose access.

- A board admin can adjust board settings under Menu > Settings > Change Visibility.

Step 4: Try a Different Browser or Device

- Access the board from a different browser or use incognito mode to check for browser-related issues.

2. Lost Access to a Card or List

If you cannot see a specific Trello card or list, it may have been:

- Archived: Go to "Show Menu" > "More" > "Archived Items" to restore it.

- Moved to another board: Ask teammates if they moved the card elsewhere.

- Deleted: Deleted cards cannot be recovered.

3. Trello Account Access Issues

If you are locked out of your Trello account, try the following:

Step 1: Reset Your Password

1. Go to the Trello login page.

2. Click **"Forgot password"** and follow the instructions.

Step 2: Check for Account Suspension

- If Trello **suspended** your account for violating policies, contact **Trello Support** for resolution.

Step 3: Ensure You Are Using the Correct Login Method

- Trello supports logins via **Google, Microsoft, Apple, or email/password**.

- If you previously logged in with Google, use **Google Sign-In** instead of entering a password manually.

Final Tips for Avoiding Notification & Access Issues

✓ Regularly check your notification settings in Trello to ensure they are enabled.

✓ Use the "Watch" feature to subscribe to important boards and cards.

✓ Keep the Trello app updated on mobile devices to avoid push notification problems.

✓ Ensure your browser and email settings allow Trello notifications.

✓ Use strong passwords and enable two-factor authentication for better security.

By following these troubleshooting steps, you can quickly resolve notification and access issues and ensure seamless collaboration with your team.

Now that you've mastered advanced troubleshooting, let's move on to more Trello best practices in the next section! 🚀

CHAPTER VII
Taking Your Trello Skills to the Next Level

7.1 Customizing Trello to Fit Your Needs

7.1.1 Creating Custom Templates

As you become more proficient in using Trello, you may find yourself repeating the same processes across different projects. Whether you're managing a team workflow, tracking personal tasks, or handling recurring projects, custom templates can help you save time and ensure consistency.

This section will guide you through why Trello templates are valuable, how to create and customize them, and best practices for using them effectively.

Why Use Trello Templates?

Trello templates are pre-designed boards, lists, or cards that can be reused whenever needed. Instead of manually setting up the same board structure over and over again, you can duplicate a template and start working instantly.

Here are some key benefits of using Trello templates:

✅ **Saves Time** – Instead of creating a new board from scratch, you can reuse a well-structured template.
✅ **Ensures Consistency** – Helps maintain a standardized workflow across different teams or projects.
✅ **Reduces Setup Errors** – Minimizes the risk of missing important steps in a process.
✅ **Scales Easily** – Templates can be adapted for multiple projects without extra effort.

☑ **Improves Collaboration** – Teams can follow a common structure, making onboarding and teamwork easier.

Now, let's walk through the process of creating custom Trello templates for boards, lists, and cards.

Creating a Custom Trello Board Template

Step 1: Set Up Your Board

Before creating a template, start by designing a board with the **structure and elements** you need.

1. **Go to Trello and create a new board**

   o Click on **"Create new board"** from the homepage.

   o Choose a **board name** that reflects its purpose (e.g., "Content Calendar Template" or "Project Management Template").

   o Select a **background** to visually distinguish it.

2. **Define Your Workflow with Lists**

   o Add lists that represent different stages of your workflow.

   o Example: If you're creating a project management board, your lists might be:

      ▪ To-Do

      ▪ In Progress

      ▪ Under Review

      ▪ Completed

3. **Add Example Cards**

   o Create sample cards to illustrate how the board should be used.

   o Include descriptions, checklists, due dates, and labels to provide guidance.

4. **Customize Labels and Tags**

- o Use color-coded labels to categorize tasks (e.g., "High Priority", "Urgent", "In Review").

- o Labels make it easier to sort and filter tasks across the board.

Step 2: Convert the Board into a Template

Once your board is fully set up, it's time to turn it into a reusable template.

1. Click on the Board Menu (Top Right Corner)

2. Select "More" → "Make template"

3. Trello will now mark the board as a template, and you'll see a new "Create board from template" button appear.

✅ Now, whenever you need to start a new project, you can create a fresh board from this template.

Creating a Custom Trello List Template

Sometimes, you may want to standardize a specific workflow within a board, rather than duplicating an entire board. In this case, you can create a reusable list template.

Step 1: Create a Model List

- Choose an existing **board** or create a new one.

- Add a **list** that you plan to use frequently (e.g., "Onboarding Checklist," "Weekly Sprint Tasks").

- Add **sample cards** with descriptions, attachments, and checklists to serve as examples.

Step 2: Copy the List for Future Use

Trello does not have a direct "Save as Template" option for lists, but you can easily duplicate lists:

1. Click on the **three-dot menu** at the top of the list.

2. Select **"Copy list"**.

3. Choose **which board to copy it to**.

4. Rename the list if necessary.

✅ This method helps you quickly reuse structured lists without manually recreating them.

Creating a Custom Trello Card Template

If you frequently create similar tasks, a card template is an excellent way to speed up the process.

Step 1: Design a Sample Card

1. Create a new card on any list.

2. Add relevant details:

   o A title that describes the task (e.g., "New Employee Onboarding Checklist").

   o A detailed description to provide instructions.

   o A checklist for step-by-step actions.

   o Attachments like PDFs, images, or reference links.

   o Labels and due dates if applicable.

Step 2: Save the Card as a Template

1. Open the card.

2. Click "Make template" (found in the card's menu).

3. The card will now be marked as a template and can be reused multiple times.

✅ Whenever you need to create a similar task, just click "Create Card from Template" and Trello will duplicate it with all predefined details.

Best Practices for Using Trello Templates Effectively

Here are some tips to make the most of your **Trello templates**:

◆ **Keep Templates Updated** – Review your templates regularly and make improvements as needed.

◆ **Use Naming Conventions** – Clearly label your templates (e.g., "Client Project Template" or "Social Media Calendar Template") so they're easy to find.

◆ **Train Your Team** – If using templates for teamwork, provide a brief guide or training to ensure everyone understands how to use them correctly.

◆ **Combine Templates with Automation** – Use **Trello Butler** to trigger automatic actions when a board, list, or card is created from a template.

Examples of Trello Templates for Different Use Cases

Still unsure how you can apply templates? Here are some examples:

◆ Project Management Board Template – A structured way to track tasks from start to finish.
◆ Content Calendar Template – Plan and organize blog posts, social media, and marketing campaigns.
◆ Sales Pipeline Template – Track leads, prospects, and closed deals.
◆ Onboarding Checklist Template – Standardize employee or client onboarding.
◆ Weekly Meeting Agenda Template – Keep track of discussion points and action items.

With Trello's flexibility, you can create templates for almost any workflow.

Final Thoughts: Why Trello Templates Are Game-Changers

Custom Trello templates empower you to work smarter, not harder. By setting up well-structured templates, you can:

✓☐ **Save time** by eliminating repetitive setup tasks.
✓☐ **Ensure consistency** across multiple projects.
✓☐ **Reduce errors** by standardizing workflows.
✓☐ **Improve collaboration** by making processes clearer for your team.

Now that you know how to create board, list, and card templates, you can customize Trello to fit your exact needs and streamline your productivity.

7.1.2 Personalizing Workflows

Trello's flexibility allows users to create personalized workflows that align with their unique needs. Whether you're managing personal tasks, team projects, or complex business processes, Trello can be customized to optimize your workflow. This section will explore various strategies for personalizing Trello workflows, including structuring boards effectively, leveraging labels and tags, automating repetitive tasks, and integrating third-party tools to enhance productivity.

Why Personalizing Workflows Matters

A well-structured workflow ensures that tasks are completed efficiently, on time, and with minimal confusion. Customizing Trello to fit your needs can help:

✓ Improve organization – Keep tasks structured in a way that makes sense for you.
✓ Boost efficiency – Reduce manual work by streamlining repetitive processes.
✓ Increase accountability – Clearly define roles and responsibilities.
✓ Enhance collaboration – Make it easier for teams to stay aligned.

Now, let's explore how you can personalize your Trello workflows to maximize productivity.

1. Designing the Perfect Board Structure

The first step in personalizing Trello workflows is setting up your boards to match your work process.

Choosing the Right Board Structure

Trello boards are highly customizable, and different board structures work best for different use cases:

- **Basic To-Do List** – Best for personal productivity (e.g., "To-Do," "In Progress," "Done").

- **Agile/Sprint Boards** – Used by development teams (e.g., "Backlog," "Sprint Planning," "In Progress," "Review," "Completed").

- **Sales and CRM Pipelines** – Ideal for tracking leads (e.g., "New Leads," "Contacted," "Follow-Up," "Closed-Won," "Closed-Lost").

- **Content Planning Boards** – Great for marketing teams (e.g., "Ideas," "Drafting," "Editing," "Scheduled," "Published").

Using Lists to Structure Workflows

Lists help categorize tasks within a board. Consider these advanced structures:

- **Deadline-Based Lists** – Organize tasks by urgency ("Today," "This Week," "Next Month").

- **Process-Based Lists** – Show a task's journey through different stages ("Requested," "Approved," "In Progress," "Completed").

- **Priority-Based Lists** – Categorize tasks by importance ("High Priority," "Medium Priority," "Low Priority").

By customizing your lists, you ensure that your Trello board mirrors your real-world workflow.

2. Enhancing Organization with Labels and Tags

Labels and tags add another layer of personalization by helping you quickly categorize tasks.

Using Color-Coded Labels

Trello allows you to assign color-coded labels to cards for easy identification. Here are a few ways to use them effectively:

- **Priority Labels** – "Urgent" (Red), "High Priority" (Orange), "Medium Priority" (Yellow), "Low Priority" (Green).

- **Task Type Labels** – "Bug Fix" (Red), "Feature Request" (Blue), "Research" (Purple).

- **Project Labels** – Assign labels based on different projects or departments.

Adding Descriptive Tags

Instead of relying only on labels, use tags or keywords in card titles (e.g., "[Client XYZ] Website Redesign – Phase 1"). This helps in quickly filtering tasks when using Trello's search functionality.

3. Automating Workflows with Butler

Trello's built-in automation tool, Butler, allows you to eliminate repetitive tasks, ensuring a smoother workflow.

Creating Automated Rules

With Butler, you can create rules that trigger specific actions when conditions are met. For example:

- **Automatically move completed tasks** → "When a card is marked as done, move it to the 'Completed' list."

- **Send reminders** → "Every Monday at 9 AM, create a new card in the 'Weekly Tasks' list."

- **Assign team members automatically** → "When a card is moved to 'In Progress,' assign it to the relevant team member."

Setting Up Custom Buttons

You can add custom buttons on Trello cards that, when clicked, perform multiple actions. Example:

🚀 **"Quick Assign" Button:**

- Adds a due date for 3 days later.

- Assigns the card to a team member.

- Moves the card to the "In Progress" list.

These small automations save time and reduce manual effort, allowing you to focus on important tasks.

4. Integrating with Other Productivity Tools

To further enhance your personalized Trello workflow, integrate it with third-party tools.

Top Trello Integrations

- **Google Calendar** → Sync due dates with your calendar for better scheduling.

- **Slack** → Get Trello updates directly in Slack for team communication.

- **Google Drive / Dropbox** → Attach files easily to Trello cards.

- **Zapier** → Automate workflows between Trello and other apps.

- **Time Tracking Tools (Toggl, Clockify)** → Track how long you spend on tasks.

These integrations help streamline workflow management, ensuring that everything is connected.

5. Using Advanced Filtering and Search

Once your Trello board is customized, finding information quickly is crucial.

Using the Trello Search Function

Trello's search is powerful and allows for advanced queries:

- Search by keyword → Type "meeting" to find all cards with "meeting" in the title.

- Filter by label → label:red (shows all high-priority tasks).

- Search by member → @john (shows all cards assigned to John).

- Filter by due date → due:week (shows tasks due this week).

Using the Board Filter Feature

If you're working on a large Trello board, use the board filter to temporarily hide irrelevant tasks:

- Filter by assigned member to see only tasks relevant to you.

- Filter by due date to focus on upcoming deadlines.

- Filter by labels to view only high-priority tasks.

These features help keep large Trello boards manageable and efficient.

Final Thoughts on Personalizing Workflows

By following these personalization strategies, you can transform Trello into a powerful and customized productivity tool that aligns with your specific workflow.

✅ Structure your boards effectively – Use lists and card organization wisely.

✅ Leverage labels and tags – Categorize and prioritize tasks easily.

✅ Automate repetitive work – Use Butler to streamline tasks.

✅ Integrate with other tools – Connect Trello with Google Drive, Slack, and more.

✅ Use filters and search – Quickly find important information.

Trello's true power lies in its adaptability. Whether you are managing a team, handling multiple projects, or just organizing your daily life, a personalized workflow can make all the difference.

💡 *In the next section, we will explore how to learn from Trello experts and communities to further enhance your skills!* 🚀

7.2 Learning from Trello Experts and Communities

7.2.1 Following Trello Best Practices

Once you have a solid understanding of how Trello works and have successfully implemented it in your daily workflow, it's time to take your skills to the next level. Many Trello experts and experienced users have refined their workflows over time and developed best practices that significantly enhance productivity and efficiency.

This section explores some of the most valuable Trello best practices that can help you optimize your workflow, increase efficiency, and collaborate more effectively.

1. Structure Your Trello Boards for Maximum Clarity

One of the key elements of an effective Trello setup is proper board organization. Whether you're using Trello for personal task management or team projects, structuring your boards correctly can improve clarity and efficiency.

Tips for Structuring Your Boards Effectively

- **Use a consistent naming convention**: Name your boards, lists, and cards in a way that makes them easy to understand at a glance. Example: Instead of a vague title like "Work Tasks," use "Q2 Marketing Campaign - To-Do List."

- **Limit the number of lists**: Avoid cluttered boards by only keeping essential lists. Too many lists can make it overwhelming to track progress.

- **Use horizontal workflow progression**: Organize lists from left to right based on workflow stages (e.g., **To-Do → In Progress → Review → Completed**).

- **Pin important boards**: Star your most frequently used boards so you can access them quickly from the **Trello dashboard.**

- **Use separate boards for large projects**: If a project involves multiple teams or departments, consider creating separate boards for each and linking them together.

A well-structured board ensures that you and your team members can navigate Trello effortlessly and locate tasks without confusion.

2. Use Labels and Tags Effectively

Labels in Trello are color-coded tags that help categorize cards, making it easier to identify tasks at a glance.

Best Practices for Using Labels in Trello

- **Use color coding consistently**: Assign specific colors to different task types. Example:

  - ● **Red** = Urgent tasks

  - ☐ **Yellow** = Tasks in progress

  - ☐ **Green** = Completed tasks

- **Use descriptive label names**: Instead of just colors, provide meaningful names like "High Priority," "Needs Review," or "Bug Fix."

- **Combine multiple labels**: Some tasks might fall under multiple categories, so use **multiple labels** when necessary.

- **Apply labels sparingly**: Avoid using too many labels, which can make a board visually overwhelming.

By using labels strategically, you can quickly filter and sort your cards to find the most relevant tasks.

3. Implement a Clear Naming Convention for Cards

When you have dozens (or hundreds) of cards in Trello, a consistent naming system makes it much easier to identify and manage tasks.

How to Name Cards Effectively

✅ **Use a structured format**: Consider using a format like [Category] Task Name - Due Date (e.g., [Marketing] Design Facebook Ads - June 15).

✅ **Add prefixes or codes**: Example: HR-01 for hiring tasks, DEV-02 for development work.

✅ **Indicate priorities in the card name**: Example: 🔥 Urgent: Fix Login Bug.

✅ **Avoid vague titles**: Instead of "Fix issue," write "Fix broken links on homepage before launch."

A good card naming system ensures that you can quickly understand the task without opening the card.

---

4. Optimize Task Management with Checklists

Checklists within Trello cards help break down larger tasks into smaller, actionable steps.

Best Practices for Using Checklists

- **Use checklists for recurring processes**: If you have tasks that follow a repetitive process (e.g., onboarding new employees), create reusable checklists.

- **Prioritize checklist items**: Move the most critical steps to the top.

- **Convert checklist items into cards**: If an individual checklist item becomes too complex, convert it into its own Trello card.

- **Use multiple checklists**: Instead of one long checklist, divide it into sections (e.g., "Pre-launch Tasks" and "Post-launch Tasks").

By incorporating checklists, you ensure that no steps are overlooked and track progress more effectively.

---

5. Utilize Due Dates and Reminders

Keeping track of deadlines is crucial, and Trello's due date feature helps ensure tasks are completed on time.

How to Use Due Dates Effectively

✓ Set realistic deadlines: Avoid overly tight or flexible deadlines—find a balance.
✓ Enable reminders: Trello sends notifications as a task's due date approaches.
✓ Color-coded due dates: Trello automatically color-codes deadlines:

- ● **Red** = Overdue

- ☐ **Yellow** = Due soon

- ☐ **Green** = Completed
  ✓ **Sort by due date**: Click "Sort" in a list to arrange tasks by due date for better prioritization.

Using due dates keeps everyone on schedule and accountable.

6. Automate Routine Tasks with Butler

Trello's Butler automation tool can save time by automating repetitive tasks.

Best Practices for Butler Automation

- Set up automatic card movements: Example: Move completed tasks to the "Done" list at the end of each week.

- Create scheduled reminders: Automatically notify team members about upcoming deadlines.

- Generate recurring tasks: Example: If a weekly report is needed, Trello can automatically create a new card every Monday.

- Use rule-based triggers: Example: If a card is marked as "Urgent," Trello can notify the project manager immediately.

By automating routine tasks, you reduce manual effort and improve efficiency.

7. Leverage Power-Ups to Extend Trello's Capabilities

Trello Power-Ups are third-party integrations that add extra functionality to your boards.

Essential Power-Ups for Trello Best Practices

♦ **Calendar View** – See tasks in a calendar format.
♦ **Google Drive** – Attach Google Docs and Sheets to cards.
♦ **Slack** – Get Trello updates in Slack channels.
♦ **Card Repeater** – Automate recurring tasks.
♦ **Time Tracking** – Track time spent on tasks.

By choosing the right Power-Ups, you can tailor Trello to your specific needs.

8. Encourage Team Collaboration and Communication

If you're using Trello in a team setting, it's important to foster a collaborative and transparent environment.

Tips for Team Collaboration

✅ Use @mentions: Tag team members in comments to keep communication clear.
✅ Pin important announcements: Use the first card in a list as a "Pinned Announcements" section.
✅ Hold regular check-ins: Use a Trello board for weekly meetings and status updates.
✅ Keep descriptions detailed: Provide enough context so others understand the task without asking questions.

Effective team collaboration ensures that everyone is on the same page and projects run smoothly.

Final Thoughts

By following these Trello best practices, you can optimize your workflow, improve productivity, and work more efficiently. Whether you're managing personal projects or collaborating in a team, these strategies will help you make the most out of Trello.

In the next section, we will explore how to learn from Trello communities and connect with experts to further enhance your skills.

7.2.2 Joining Online Trello Communities

Trello is more than just a task management tool—it has a thriving community of users, experts, and enthusiasts who share their knowledge, best practices, and creative ways to use Trello. By joining online Trello communities, you can stay updated on new features, get troubleshooting help, learn advanced techniques, and discover innovative use cases that you might not have thought of before.

In this section, we will explore:

- The benefits of joining online Trello communities

- The best platforms to find and engage with Trello users

- How to get the most value from these communities

- A few success stories from real Trello users who improved their workflow through community involvement

Let's dive into why online communities can help take your Trello skills to the next level.

Why Join an Online Trello Community?

Becoming part of an online Trello community offers many advantages, whether you're a beginner looking for guidance or an advanced user seeking new productivity hacks.

1. Get Help and Troubleshoot Issues Quickly

If you ever encounter an issue in Trello—whether it's a technical bug, confusion about a feature, or uncertainty about how to structure your boards—online communities are the perfect place to find solutions.

- Experienced users and Trello enthusiasts actively answer questions, providing quick responses and workarounds.

- Many Trello experts share tutorials, templates, and real-world solutions that can help you optimize your setup.

- If you can't find an answer, you can post your question and receive guidance from people who have faced similar challenges.

2. Learn New Productivity Techniques

One of the best reasons to join a Trello community is to learn from others. People use Trello in unique and creative ways, and by engaging with a community, you can discover innovative methods to streamline your workflow.

For example, you might learn:

✅ How to use Trello for personal productivity (habit tracking, daily planning, journaling)

✅ How companies use Trello for agile project management

✅ How to integrate Trello with automation tools like Butler, Zapier, or Slack

✅ How to set up advanced workflows using power-ups and integrations

3. Stay Updated on Trello's Latest Features and Updates

Trello is constantly evolving, with new features, power-ups, and interface changes being introduced regularly. Community groups are one of the best places to stay informed about updates and learn how to use them effectively.

- Trello's official team members often post about upcoming features and improvements.

- Early adopters share their reviews and experiences with new updates.

- Users provide feedback and suggestions that Trello may consider in future updates.

4. Expand Your Network and Connect with Like-Minded Users

By engaging in Trello communities, you connect with professionals, project managers, freelancers, and productivity enthusiasts who share similar interests.

- You can network with industry experts who use Trello in your field.

- If you're a freelancer or consultant, you can find potential clients or collaborators.

- If you love sharing knowledge, you can build a reputation as a Trello expert by helping others.

5. Access Free Trello Resources

Many Trello communities offer free resources such as:

- Pre-made Trello board templates for different use cases.

- Tutorials, eBooks, and webinars on Trello best practices.

- Cheat sheets and keyboard shortcuts for faster navigation.

Now that we've explored the benefits, let's look at where you can find these communities.

The Best Online Trello Communities to Join

There are many places online where Trello users gather to share tips, discuss ideas, and solve problems together. Below are some of the best platforms where you can engage with Trello users.

1. Trello Community Forum (Official Atlassian Community)

🔖 **Website**: https://community.atlassian.com/t5/Trello/ct-p/trello

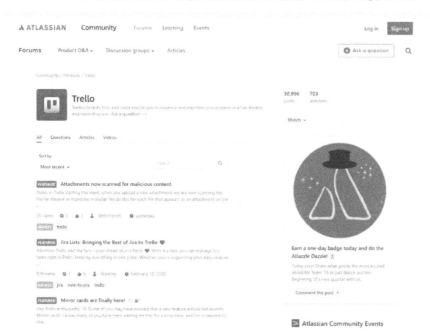

Trello's official community forum, hosted by Atlassian, is the best place to ask questions, share knowledge, and connect with other Trello users.

✅ **Key features**:

- Direct interaction with Trello staff members.

- Discussion categories covering how-to guides, troubleshooting, and best practices.

- Announcements on new features, updates, and beta programs.

2. Trello Subreddit (r/Trello)

📍 **Website:** https://www.reddit.com/r/trello

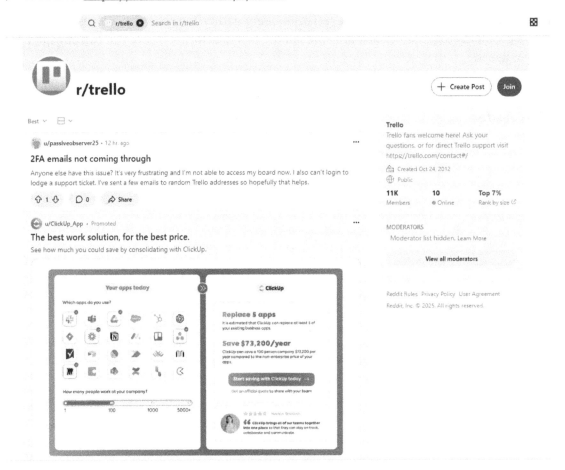

Reddit is home to one of the most active Trello user communities. The r/Trello subreddit is a place where users ask questions, share workflow ideas, and showcase their Trello setups.

✅ **Key features:**

- Casual discussions about real-world Trello applications.

- People share custom board templates and automation tricks.

- Engaged users help troubleshoot common issues and technical questions.

3. Facebook Groups for Trello Users

There are several Facebook groups dedicated to Trello users, where members actively share tips, tricks, and resources.

◆ Popular Groups:

- Trello Productivity Tips & Tricks

- Project Management with Trello

- Trello for Business Owners & Entrepreneurs

These groups are excellent for networking, asking questions, and seeing how others use Trello in their daily work.

4. Trello on LinkedIn

🔎 Search for "Trello Users" or "Trello Productivity" on LinkedIn

LinkedIn is a great place to find professional groups where business users discuss Trello for project management, team collaboration, and productivity.

✅ Key benefits:

- Engage with professionals who use Trello in corporate settings.

- Stay updated on how companies integrate Trello with business tools.

- Find Trello webinars, live discussions, and expert panels.

5. YouTube Channels and Discord Communities

- YouTube: Search for "Trello tutorials" to find step-by-step guides and advanced workflow ideas.

- Discord Servers: Some online communities have Trello-related Discord servers where users discuss in real-time.

How to Get the Most Value from Online Trello Communities

1. Engage Actively

- Don't just observe—ask questions, participate in discussions, and share your insights.

- Reply to others' questions if you have relevant experience.

2. Share Your Trello Boards and Workflows

- Show how you organize your projects, tasks, or team workflows.

- Ask for feedback to improve your system.

3. Stay Open to Learning

- Keep up with new techniques and community discoveries.

- Try out recommended power-ups and integrations.

4. Contribute to the Community

- If you become experienced in Trello, consider creating tutorials or templates to help others.

- Become a trusted member and grow your professional network.

Final Thoughts

Joining an online Trello community is one of the fastest ways to level up your skills. Whether you're looking for troubleshooting help, new workflow ideas, or productivity hacks, these communities provide endless opportunities to learn and connect with like-minded users.

By staying active in these groups, you can maximize the potential of Trello, stay ahead of new features, and continuously improve your task management skills.

Next, we'll explore how you can expand your productivity beyond Trello and build long-term habits for better task management!

7.3 Expanding Your Productivity Beyond Trello

Trello is an incredible tool for organizing tasks, managing projects, and collaborating with teams. However, true productivity is not just about using one tool effectively—it's about creating a seamless workflow that integrates multiple tools to optimize efficiency.

In this section, we will explore other productivity tools that complement Trello, helping you automate tasks, enhance collaboration, manage time effectively, and improve overall workflow.

7.3.1 Exploring Other Productivity Tools

While Trello excels at visual task management, there are many other specialized productivity tools that can enhance different aspects of your work. These tools can be used alongside Trello to improve collaboration, time tracking, document management, communication, and automation.

Let's explore some of the best tools that work well with Trello and help you take your productivity to the next level.

Time Management and Task Scheduling Tools

Managing time efficiently is a crucial part of productivity. Trello helps you organize your tasks, but combining it with time management tools can ensure that your work gets done on schedule.

☐ **Toggl Track (Time Tracking)**

- A simple and powerful time-tracking tool that helps you track how much time you spend on tasks.

- Easily integrate Toggl with Trello to start and stop timers directly from your Trello cards.

- Provides detailed reports to help you analyze productivity trends.

🏬 Google Calendar (Task Scheduling & Reminders)

- Helps you schedule tasks and set deadlines with reminders.

- Integrates with Trello, allowing you to sync due dates from Trello cards to your calendar.

- Perfect for scheduling meetings, deadlines, and personal tasks.

☐ RescueTime (Productivity Analysis)

- Tracks how much time you spend on different apps and websites.

- Provides detailed insights into your work habits and helps you eliminate distractions.

- Can be used alongside Trello to measure your actual productivity.

Collaboration and Communication Tools

While Trello is great for task management, communication is key when working in a team. These tools can help enhance team discussions and streamline collaboration.

💬 Slack (Team Messaging & Communication)

- A powerful real-time messaging app that integrates with Trello.

- Get notifications when a Trello card is updated.

- Allows teams to discuss tasks and projects without endless email threads.

📞 Zoom (Virtual Meetings & Video Conferencing)

- Useful for remote teams that need regular video meetings.

- Can be used alongside Trello to discuss tasks, brainstorm ideas, and resolve issues.

- Schedule Zoom meetings directly from Trello cards.

📧 Microsoft Outlook & Gmail (Email Communication)

- Trello integrates with both Outlook and Gmail to help you turn emails into Trello tasks.

- Useful for managing customer support, sales, and project-related emails.

File Storage and Documentation Tools

Trello allows you to attach files, but when dealing with large volumes of documents, it's best to use a dedicated cloud storage and documentation tool.

💼 Google Drive & Dropbox (Cloud Storage & File Sharing)

- Store and manage files directly from your Trello cards.

- Ideal for teams handling project files, contracts, reports, and media assets.

- Helps keep Trello boards organized and decluttered.

📋 Notion & Evernote (Advanced Note-Taking & Documentation)

- While Trello is great for managing tasks, Notion and Evernote are perfect for storing notes, meeting summaries, and research materials.

- Use them alongside Trello to document important project details.

- Create knowledge bases and project wikis for your team.

Automation and Workflow Optimization Tools

Automating repetitive tasks can save time and reduce human errors. The following tools help streamline your workflow when used alongside Trello.

☐ Zapier (Workflow Automation)

- Connects Trello with thousands of apps to automate tasks.

- Example: Automatically create Trello cards from emails or update Google Sheets when a Trello task is completed.

- Saves hours by reducing manual work.

⚙☐ Butler for Trello (Built-in Trello Automation)

- Helps automate Trello workflows without needing external apps.

- Example: Move cards automatically when a checklist is completed or assign tasks based on due dates.

- Reduces the time spent on managing Trello boards manually.

Advanced Project Management Tools

For larger teams or complex projects, Trello might need to be combined with more robust project management software.

📊 Asana (Project & Task Management)

- Similar to Trello but with more detailed task dependencies and project timelines.

- Can be integrated with Trello to combine both visual and structured task management.

- Great for teams working on long-term projects with multiple phases.

📈 Monday.com (Workflow & Resource Management)

- Provides a visual representation of team progress and project milestones.

- Can be used alongside Trello for tracking workloads and resource allocation.

- Works well for businesses managing multiple departments.

Choosing the Right Tools for Your Workflow

With so many options available, how do you choose the best tools to use alongside Trello? Here's a simple approach:

1. **Identify your pain points** – Are you struggling with communication, time tracking, or automation?

2. **Test different tools** – Most productivity tools offer free trials, so experiment before committing.

3. **Ensure compatibility** – Pick tools that integrate with Trello to avoid switching between platforms manually.

4. **Keep it simple** – Don't overload yourself with too many tools—focus on what truly enhances your workflow.

Final Thoughts on Expanding Your Productivity Beyond Trello

Trello is an exceptional tool, but true productivity comes from creating an ecosystem of tools that complement each other. By integrating Trello with time management, collaboration, automation, and documentation tools, you can build an efficient, seamless workflow that enhances your productivity.

✓ Time Tracking & Scheduling: Toggl, Google Calendar, RescueTime
✓ Collaboration & Communication: Slack, Zoom, Gmail, Outlook
✓ File Storage & Documentation: Google Drive, Dropbox, Notion, Evernote
✓ Automation & Optimization: Zapier, Butler for Trello
✓ Advanced Project Management: Asana, Monday.com

By combining the right tools with Trello, you can work smarter, save time, and achieve more with less effort.

Next Steps: Building Long-Term Productivity Habits

Now that you understand how to expand your productivity beyond Trello, the next section will focus on developing long-term habits for effective task management and workflow optimization.

7.3.2 Building Long-Term Habits for Task Management

Using Trello effectively is a great step toward organizing tasks and improving productivity. However, true productivity is not just about using a tool—it's about building sustainable habits that help you stay organized, focused, and efficient over the long run.

Developing good task management habits ensures that you consistently meet deadlines, prioritize effectively, and manage workloads without feeling overwhelmed. In this section, we will explore the key long-term habits that will help you maximize the benefits of Trello while creating a strong foundation for lifelong productivity.

1. Develop a Daily and Weekly Review Routine

One of the most effective ways to maintain long-term productivity is to establish a consistent review routine for your Trello boards. A structured review system helps ensure that your tasks are always up to date and aligned with your goals.

Daily Review

A 5-10 minute daily review of your Trello board can keep you on track and prevent tasks from piling up.

- Check your priority tasks: Look at today's tasks and adjust priorities if needed.

- Update card statuses: Move cards between lists to reflect progress.

- Clear completed tasks: Archive or mark tasks as done to keep your board organized.

- Add new tasks: If any new tasks come up, add them to your backlog or appropriate list.

- Set intentions: Identify the top three tasks you need to complete that day.

Weekly Review

A 30-60 minute weekly review allows you to reflect on your progress and plan ahead.

- Look back at completed tasks: Evaluate what you accomplished and identify any unfinished work.

- Plan for the next week: Move tasks to the appropriate lists based on their priority.

- Adjust deadlines: Reschedule tasks as necessary to maintain a realistic workflow.

- Declutter your board: Remove unnecessary tasks, consolidate lists, or reorganize for better clarity.

By making these review routines a habit, you'll always have a clear picture of what needs to be done, ensuring better organization and productivity.

2. Prioritize Tasks Effectively with the Eisenhower Matrix

One of the biggest challenges in task management is deciding which tasks to work on first. Without a proper system, it's easy to get overwhelmed by low-priority tasks while neglecting important ones.

To avoid this, use the Eisenhower Matrix, a powerful decision-making tool that categorizes tasks into four quadrants:

1. Urgent & Important → Do immediately

2. Important but Not Urgent → Schedule for later

3. Urgent but Not Important → Delegate to someone else

4. Neither Urgent nor Important → Eliminate or postpone

How to Apply This in Trello:

- Create labels to categorize tasks based on urgency and importance.

- Assign due dates and reminders for important tasks so they don't get overlooked.

- Delegate non-essential tasks to team members using Trello's "Assign Members" feature.

- Regularly review and move low-priority tasks to the backlog to prevent unnecessary distractions.

By consistently prioritizing using the Eisenhower Matrix, you ensure that your time and energy are spent on what truly matters.

3. Break Large Projects into Manageable Steps

A common mistake in task management is setting vague or overly large tasks that seem overwhelming. The key to staying productive in the long run is breaking down big projects into smaller, actionable steps.

How to Do This in Trello:

- **Use checklists**: Instead of one large task, create a checklist with step-by-step actions.

- **Break projects into phases**: Create multiple lists for different project stages (e.g., Planning → Execution → Review).

- **Use subtasks**: Attach related Trello cards to track detailed steps.

By breaking tasks into smaller, manageable pieces, you'll feel less overwhelmed and make steady progress toward your goals.

4. Automate Repetitive Workflows

Long-term productivity is about working smarter, not harder. One of the best ways to do this is to automate repetitive tasks so you can focus on more meaningful work.

How to Use Trello for Automation:

- Set up **Butler rules** to move tasks automatically based on due dates.

- Create **templates** for frequently repeated projects or workflows.

- Use **recurring tasks** for weekly or monthly responsibilities (e.g., report submissions).

- Integrate Trello with **Zapier or IFTTT** to automate actions between different apps.

With automation, you'll save time and energy, allowing you to focus on high-value work.

5. Maintain a Healthy Work-Life Balance

Being productive doesn't mean working all the time—it means working efficiently while maintaining balance. Sustainable productivity requires avoiding burnout and ensuring that you have time to recharge.

Strategies to Maintain Balance:

- **Set boundaries**: Use Trello's scheduling features to avoid overloading yourself with tasks.

- **Time blocking**: Plan focused work periods with breaks in between.

- **Use Trello for personal goals**: Create boards for hobbies, fitness, or self-care to ensure a well-rounded life.

- **Take regular breaks**: Apply the Pomodoro Technique (work 25 minutes, break 5 minutes) to stay refreshed.

When you maintain a balanced lifestyle, your long-term productivity increases, and you'll feel more motivated to keep using Trello effectively.

6. Continually Improve Your System

No task management system is perfect from the start. Over time, your workflow will evolve, and it's important to adapt Trello to your changing needs.

Ways to Continuously Improve:

- **Experiment with different board structures**: Try different layouts to see what works best for you.

- **Adopt new Trello features**: Stay updated with Trello's latest tools and improvements.

- **Learn from others**: Join online Trello communities or watch tutorials for fresh ideas.

- **Review your productivity metrics**: Track your progress and adjust strategies as needed.

By making continuous improvement a habit, you'll ensure that your task management system remains efficient and serves your needs in the long run.

Final Thoughts

Building long-term task management habits is the key to sustaining productivity and efficiency beyond just using Trello. While Trello provides the tools to manage work, your habits determine how effective you will be in the long run.

To summarize:

✓ Review your Trello boards daily and weekly for better organization.

✓ Prioritize tasks using the Eisenhower Matrix to focus on what truly matters.

✓ Break down large tasks into smaller steps to avoid feeling overwhelmed.

✓ Automate repetitive work to save time and energy.

✓ Maintain a healthy work-life balance to prevent burnout.

✓ Continuously refine your Trello system to adapt to changing needs.

By incorporating these habits into your routine, you will be able to maximize productivity, stay organized, and manage your tasks efficiently—both inside and outside of Trello.

In the next section, we will wrap up everything we've learned in this book and explore the next steps to keep improving your Trello skills. 🚀

Conclusion

8.1 Recap of Key Takeaways

As we reach the conclusion of *Trello for Beginners: Master Task Management with Ease*, it's time to reflect on everything we've learned throughout this book. Trello is more than just a simple task management tool—it is a powerful, flexible, and intuitive platform that can help individuals and teams organize their work, enhance collaboration, and improve productivity.

In this section, we will revisit the key concepts, strategies, and best practices covered in the previous chapters to reinforce your understanding of Trello and ensure you have a solid foundation for using it effectively. Whether you're managing projects for work, tracking personal goals, or organizing your daily tasks, Trello can be adapted to fit your unique needs.

Getting Started with Trello

In **Chapter 1**, we introduced you to Trello, explaining what it is, how it works, and why it is such a valuable tool for task management. Here are the essential takeaways:

- **Trello is a visual task management tool** that uses boards, lists, and cards to help users organize work.

- **Setting up a Trello account is simple**, and navigating the interface is intuitive, making it easy for beginners to get started.

- **The Kanban method** is the foundation of Trello's structure, enabling users to track tasks through different stages of completion.

- Trello's interface consists of:

    o **Boards**, which represent a project or workflow.

    o **Lists**, which categorize different stages of a project.

- o **Cards**, which represent tasks or actionable items.

- **Trello's real-time updates** and **drag-and-drop functionality** make it a dynamic and user-friendly tool for task management.

If you ever feel lost, remember that Trello's interface is **designed for simplicity**, and with a bit of practice, navigating the platform will become second nature.

Understanding Trello's Core Features

To **fully harness the power of Trello**, you need to understand its core features, which were covered in **Chapter 2**. Here's a recap of the essential features:

- **Boards**: The central workspace where your projects are managed. You can create multiple boards for different areas of your life or work.

- **Lists**: These help organize tasks within a board, often structured as "To-Do," "In Progress," and "Done."

- **Cards**: Individual tasks that can contain descriptions, attachments, checklists, labels, and more.

- **Labels and Tags**: Customizable color-coded labels help categorize and prioritize tasks.

- **Due Dates and Reminders**: Set deadlines for tasks and receive notifications when due dates are approaching.

- **Checklists**: Break down complex tasks into smaller, manageable steps.

- **Card Assignments**: Assign team members to specific tasks to clarify responsibilities.

By mastering these features, you can effectively organize your work and keep track of progress.

Collaboration and Teamwork in Trello

Trello is not just for individual productivity—it is also a powerful **collaboration tool for teams**, as discussed in **Chapter 3**. Key points include:

- **Team Collaboration**: Multiple users can work on the same board, making it easy to share information, assign tasks, and track progress.

- **Comments and Mentions**: Team members can communicate directly on Trello cards, reducing the need for excessive emails.

- **File Attachments**: Documents, images, and other files can be uploaded to cards for easy access.

- **Trello Workspaces**: Organizations and teams can group multiple boards together for better management.

If you work in a team environment, leveraging Trello's collaboration features will help streamline communication and improve overall efficiency.

Advanced Features and Automation

In **Chapter 4**, we explored Trello's advanced functionalities, including automation, integrations, and Power-Ups. Here are the highlights:

- **Butler Automation**:
  - Create custom rules to automate repetitive tasks.
  - Set up scheduled commands for recurring activities.
  - Use buttons and triggers to enhance workflow efficiency.

- **Power-Ups**:
  - Extend Trello's functionality by integrating with tools like Google Drive, Slack, Jira, and Evernote.
  - Use the Calendar Power-Up to visualize due dates.
  - Enable time tracking Power-Ups for better project tracking.

By automating repetitive tasks and integrating Trello with other tools, you can maximize efficiency and reduce manual work.

Optimizing Trello for Different Use Cases

Trello is incredibly versatile, as shown in **Chapter 5**, where we explored different **use cases and workflows**. Key takeaways include:

- **Personal Productivity**: Using Trello for goal setting, habit tracking, and daily task management.

- **Project Management**: Creating structured workflows for managing complex projects.

- **Agile & Scrum**: Implementing Trello for software development and sprint planning.

- **Content Planning**: Managing editorial calendars and social media scheduling.

- **Event Planning**: Organizing conferences, weddings, and meetings.

Understanding how Trello can be adapted to different workflows allows you to customize it to fit your unique needs.

Expanding Your Productivity Beyond Trello

In **Chapter 7**, we discussed how Trello can be combined with other tools and best practices to **further enhance your productivity**. Key insights include:

- Customizing Trello to fit your workflow with templates, labels, and automation.

- Learning from Trello experts by joining online communities, reading blogs, and following best practices.

- Exploring additional productivity tools like Notion, Asana, or Evernote to complement Trello.

- Building long-term habits for productivity, such as time blocking, prioritization, and structured workflows.

Trello is a fantastic tool, but true productivity comes from consistent habits and a structured approach to task management.

Final Thoughts on Using Trello Effectively

To summarize, here are the core principles of using Trello effectively:

✅ Keep it simple – Start with a basic structure and gradually expand as needed.

✅ Stay organized – Use labels, checklists, and due dates to manage tasks efficiently.

✅ Collaborate effectively – Assign team members, leave comments, and share files.

✅ Automate repetitive tasks – Use Butler to streamline workflows.

✅ Customize to fit your needs – Adapt Trello for personal or professional use.

✅ Keep learning and improving – Stay engaged with Trello communities and best practices.

Mastering Trello is not just about learning the tool—it's about adopting the right mindset and strategies to manage work effectively.

In the next section, we'll explore how you can continue improving your Trello skills and stay ahead in task management.

Final Words

We've covered a lot throughout this book, and by now, you should feel confident in using Trello to organize your work and increase productivity.

Trello is a tool that grows with you. The more you use it, the more you'll discover ways to optimize your workflow and improve efficiency.

As you continue your Trello journey, don't be afraid to experiment, try new approaches, and refine your system.

8.2 How to Keep Improving Your Trello Skills

Mastering Trello is not a one-time achievement—it's an ongoing process. As Trello continues to evolve and as your workflow changes, there are always new ways to refine your skills and optimize how you use the platform. Whether you're using Trello for personal organization, team collaboration, or business project management, continuously improving your skills can significantly boost your productivity and efficiency.

This section explores various strategies to help you keep learning, stay updated with Trello's latest features, and develop advanced techniques to maximize your use of the platform.

Staying Updated with Trello's Latest Features

Trello is constantly improving, adding new features and integrations that enhance user experience. To ensure you're using Trello to its full potential, it's important to stay informed about these updates.

Ways to Keep Up with Trello Updates

- **Follow Trello's Official Blog and Newsletters**

  o Trello regularly publishes updates, feature announcements, and best practices on their official blog.

  o Subscribing to Trello's newsletter can help you receive important updates directly in your inbox.

- **Check Trello's Product Roadmap**

  o Atlassian, Trello's parent company, maintains a public roadmap showing upcoming changes and feature releases.

  o Monitoring the roadmap helps you prepare for new capabilities that might improve your workflow.

- **Enable In-App Feature Notifications**

○ Trello often announces new features through in-app notifications. Keeping an eye on these alerts ensures you don't miss important updates.

By staying informed, you can take advantage of new tools and enhancements as soon as they become available.

Practicing and Experimenting with Advanced Features

The best way to improve your Trello skills is through continuous practice. While you may already be comfortable with the basics, there are several advanced features worth exploring.

Advanced Trello Features to Master

- **Custom Fields**: Add extra information to cards by creating custom fields (e.g., priority levels, project stages, estimated completion times).

- **Butler Automation**: Learn how to automate repetitive tasks by creating custom rules, scheduled commands, and card actions.

- **Power-Ups**: Experiment with Trello Power-Ups, which allow you to extend Trello's functionality (e.g., Gantt charts, time tracking, advanced reporting).

- **Calendar and Timeline Views**: Use different Trello views to visualize your projects in new ways, making long-term planning easier.

To improve, set a goal to try one new feature each week and experiment with how it fits into your workflow.

Learning from Trello Experts and the Community

Trello has a global community of users who share insights, workflows, and best practices. Engaging with the Trello community can help you learn advanced techniques and find creative ways to use the platform.

Where to Connect with Other Trello Users

- **Trello Community Forums**

- Join the official Trello forums to ask questions, share tips, and connect with power users.

- **LinkedIn Groups and Facebook Communities**

  - Many professionals share their Trello experiences and strategies in dedicated online groups.

- **YouTube Tutorials and Webinars**

  - Follow Trello experts who create video content explaining advanced tips and tricks.

- **Reddit (r/Trello)**

  - A popular space where users discuss innovative ways to use Trello in different industries.

By learning from others, you can discover new strategies to streamline your workflow and solve common productivity challenges.

Taking Online Courses and Training

If you want to take your Trello skills to the next level, consider investing time in formal training.

Best Ways to Learn Trello Through Courses

- **Udemy, Coursera, and LinkedIn Learning**

  - These platforms offer structured Trello courses, from beginner to advanced levels.

- **Atlassian University**

  - Atlassian, Trello's parent company, provides official training courses on Trello and its integrations.

- **Company Training Programs**

o   Many businesses offer internal Trello workshops to improve productivity across teams.

Online courses often include practical exercises and real-world case studies, helping you apply what you learn directly to your work.

Developing a Systematic Approach to Task Management

As you improve your Trello skills, it's important to focus on developing a system that consistently works for you. This means refining your workflow, organizing your boards effectively, and ensuring that Trello enhances—not complicates—your productivity.

Tips for Optimizing Your Trello System

- **Standardize Board Structures**: Define clear list categories (e.g., "To Do," "In Progress," "Completed") to maintain consistency.

- **Use Labels and Tags Effectively**: Create a simple labeling system that makes it easy to filter and find tasks.

- **Limit Work in Progress (WIP)**: Avoid overwhelming yourself by capping the number of tasks in progress at any time.

- **Regularly Review and Archive**: Conduct weekly or monthly reviews to clean up old cards and ensure everything stays organized.

By **fine-tuning** how you use Trello, you'll prevent clutter and ensure that your system remains **efficient** over time.

Exploring Trello Alternatives and Complementary Tools

Even though Trello is a powerful tool, it might not cover all your project management needs. Understanding its limitations and learning how to integrate it with other tools can further enhance your productivity.

Complementary Tools to Use with Trello

- **Trello + Slack**: Use Slack notifications to get real-time updates on Trello activities.

- **Trello + Google Calendar**: Sync Trello with Google Calendar to keep track of deadlines.

- **Trello + Notion or Evernote**: Use Notion or Evernote for detailed note-taking while managing tasks in Trello.

- **Trello + Jira**: If you work in software development, integrating Trello with Jira can help bridge the gap between task management and bug tracking.

Understanding how to integrate multiple productivity tools can help you build a more powerful and efficient workflow.

Making Trello a Habit for Long-Term Productivity

The key to truly mastering Trello is making it a habit rather than just a tool you occasionally use.

How to Make Trello Part of Your Daily Routine

- **Start and End Your Day with Trello**

  - Begin each day by reviewing your Trello board and planning your top priorities.

  - At the end of the day, update the board and move completed tasks accordingly.

- **Schedule Weekly Reviews**

  - Take time once a week to organize your tasks, adjust deadlines, and clear out unnecessary items.

- **Encourage Team Adoption**

  - If you work with a team, promote Trello as a shared workspace to enhance collaboration.

By making Trello a consistent part of your workflow, it becomes an indispensable productivity tool.

Final Thoughts: Keep Learning and Adapting

Trello is an incredibly versatile tool, but the real power comes from how you use it. To keep improving:

✓ **Stay updated** with Trello's latest features.

✓ **Experiment** with advanced functions like Butler automation and Power-Ups.

✓ **Engage** with the Trello community to learn best practices.

✓ **Invest** in structured learning through courses and training.

✓ **Refine** your workflow and explore complementary productivity tools.

By continuously adapting and learning, you can transform Trello from a simple task manager into a powerful system that maximizes your productivity and helps you stay organized effortlessly.

🚀 Now, take what you've learned and start mastering Trello like a pro!

8.3 Final Thoughts and Encouragement

As we reach the final section of *Trello for Beginners: Master Task Management with Ease*, it's time to reflect on the journey you've taken in learning how to effectively use Trello. From setting up your first board to customizing workflows and automating repetitive tasks, you have gained the foundational knowledge needed to manage tasks, collaborate with teams, and stay organized using Trello.

But the journey doesn't stop here. Mastering Trello—or any productivity tool—is an ongoing process. Trello is designed to be flexible, scalable, and adaptable to various needs, whether you're a student organizing assignments, a professional managing projects, or a business owner streamlining operations. As you continue using Trello, you'll discover new ways to refine your workflow, improve efficiency, and make the tool work even better for you.

In this final section, let's recap some essential lessons, explore strategies for continuous improvement, and leave you with encouragement to make the most of your Trello experience.

Reflecting on Your Trello Journey

Looking back at what you've learned, Trello offers:

- A visual and intuitive task management system that makes it easy to organize projects.

- A collaborative workspace that keeps teams aligned and on track.

- Customizable workflows that can adapt to any industry or personal need.

- Powerful integrations with other tools to enhance productivity.

- Automation features that reduce repetitive work and save time.

If you started this book as a complete beginner, you've now reached a point where you can confidently navigate Trello, create structured workflows, and maximize your efficiency. The key to continued success lies in applying what you've learned consistently and refining your approach as you go.

Tip: If you ever feel overwhelmed, remember that Trello is designed to be simple. Start small, master the basics, and gradually explore more advanced features over time.

Overcoming Common Challenges

Like any tool, Trello has a learning curve. You might encounter obstacles along the way, but these challenges are opportunities for growth. Here are some common difficulties new users face and ways to overcome them:

Feeling Overwhelmed with Too Many Features

Trello offers numerous features, but you don't need to use them all at once. Start with a basic Kanban board (To-Do, In Progress, Done) and gradually introduce labels, checklists, and automation when necessary.

Struggling with Team Collaboration

If your team isn't fully engaged with Trello, make sure everyone understands how to use it effectively. Consider:

- Conducting a brief onboarding session for new team members.
- Setting clear guidelines for board organization and task assignments.
- Using Trello's comment and mention system to enhance communication.

Difficulty Maintaining Long-Term Productivity

Many people start using Trello with enthusiasm but later struggle to maintain consistency. To stay on track:

- Schedule weekly reviews to clean up old tasks and update priorities.
- Use automation (Butler) to remind you of deadlines and repetitive tasks.
- Keep your boards organized and decluttered to prevent distractions.

Remember: Productivity isn't just about using the right tools—it's about building the right habits.

Strategies for Continuous Improvement

The best Trello users are those who constantly refine their processes. Here are some ways you can keep improving:

Experiment with New Workflows

Try different list structures to find what works best for your projects. For example:

- Kanban-style boards (To-Do, In Progress, Done) for task tracking.
- Editorial calendars for content planning.
- CRM boards for managing clients and sales pipelines.

Stay Updated with Trello's Latest Features

Trello continuously releases updates and new features. Keep an eye on:

- Trello's official blog and community forums.
- Webinars and tutorials by Trello experts.
- New integrations that improve your workflow.

Engage with the Trello Community

Join Trello communities on platforms like Reddit, Facebook, or Trello's own forum to:

- Learn from other experienced users.
- Get inspiration from real-world use cases.
- Ask for troubleshooting tips and best practices.

Teach Others and Reinforce Your Knowledge

One of the best ways to master a tool is to teach others. Whether it's training a colleague, writing a blog post about your Trello experience, or even just explaining a feature to a friend, sharing knowledge will deepen your own understanding.

Action Step: Challenge yourself to teach one person how to use Trello in the next month!

Final Words of Encouragement

As you step forward with your newfound Trello skills, remember that productivity is a journey, not a destination. Trello is just a tool—how you use it depends on your habits, mindset, and commitment to continuous improvement.

Believe in Progress, Not Perfection

You don't have to get everything right immediately. Start with small improvements and refine your process over time. Even the most experienced Trello users are still learning and adjusting their workflows.

Stay Curious and Keep Exploring

Don't be afraid to explore new Trello features, try different board setups, and customize your workflow. The more you experiment, the better you'll become at managing your tasks effectively.

Celebrate Your Wins

Recognize your progress! Whether it's completing a major project, improving team collaboration, or simply keeping your tasks more organized, every small win is worth celebrating.

You're in Control of Your Productivity

Trello is a powerful tool, but the real power lies in how you use it. Take ownership of your productivity, stay disciplined, and make Trello work for you.

🚀 **Your next step?** Go apply what you've learned! Start by reviewing your current Trello boards, optimizing your workflow, and setting clear goals for how you want to improve.

A Heartfelt Thank You!

Thank you for taking the time to read *Trello for Beginners: Master Task Management with Ease*! I hope this book has provided you with valuable insights, practical techniques, and the confidence to use Trello effectively.

If you found this guide helpful, consider sharing it with friends, colleagues, or anyone who could benefit from better task management. And if you ever need a refresher, you can always revisit these pages to reinforce your knowledge.

Now, go forth and **conquer your tasks with Trello!** 💡 🎯 🔥

Final Thought: *The best productivity system is the one that works for you. Keep refining, keep learning, and keep growing!*

Acknowledgments

Thank You for Reading!

First and foremost, I want to sincerely thank you for choosing *Trello for Beginners: Master Task Management with Ease*. I know that there are countless productivity tools and guides available, so I truly appreciate you investing your time in this book. My goal was to provide you with a clear, practical, and easy-to-follow guide to mastering Trello, and I hope that it has helped you feel more confident in organizing your tasks and projects.

Writing this book has been a journey of learning, discovery, and refinement. Throughout the process, I have drawn inspiration from the many Trello users around the world who continuously find innovative ways to boost their productivity. If this book has made even a small positive impact on your workflow, then my efforts have been worthwhile.

I am also incredibly grateful to all the productivity enthusiasts, Trello experts, and members of the Trello community who share their insights, tips, and best practices. Your creativity and dedication to efficiency have played a significant role in shaping the content of this book.

A special thank you to my readers—whether you are a student, a professional, an entrepreneur, or simply someone looking to bring more organization into your daily life. Your commitment to improving your workflow and optimizing your time is truly inspiring. I hope that this book serves as a valuable resource for you, not just today but for years to come.

Finally, if you found this book helpful, I would love to hear from you! Your feedback, reviews, and stories about how Trello has transformed your productivity mean the world to me. Feel free to connect with me through social media, email, or online communities—I always enjoy learning from fellow productivity enthusiasts.

Thank you once again for your support and for allowing me to be part of your Trello journey. Now, go out there and take control of your tasks, streamline your workflow, and make the most of every day!

Wishing you success and productivity,

www.ingramcontent.com/pod-product-compliance
Lightning Source LLC
Chambersburg PA
CBHW080359060326
40689CB00019B/4067